GRACEFUL POWER

Solving the paradox of modern leadership

SALLY NETHERWOOD

First published in Great Britain by Practical Inspiration Publishing, 2026

ISBN 9781788606493 (paperback)
9781788606486 (hardback)
9781788606516 (epub)

EU GPSR representative: LOGOS EUROPE, 9 rue Nicolas Poussin, LA ROCHELLE 17000, France Contact@logoseurope.eu

Want to bulk-buy copies of this book for your team and colleagues? We can customize the content and co-brand *Graceful Power* to suit your business's needs.

Please email info@practicalinspiration.com for more details.

Sally brings a rare ability to help leaders harness both power and grace – a balance the world urgently needs. Having benefited from Sally's approach personally, I know it's impact first-hand. *Graceful Power* distils her wisdom into a compelling guide for anyone striving to lead with strength, purpose and integrity.

Ariane Gorin, Chief Executive Officer at Expedia Group

I've had the privilege of being coached by Sally, the absolute best in leadership coaching. Her impact on my ability to lead powerfully, unite teams and evolve as a person has been immense. She has a brilliant, compassionate style and understands how to guide leaders to uncover the answers to their most pressing questions. What a gift that this is now captured in a book for so many more leaders to benefit from.

Tyler Turnbull, Global Chief Executive Officer at McCann

Sally Netherwood was a truth-teller and a steady force in my life when I needed it most. Her guidance didn't just help me lead – it helped me lead in a way that was powerful, human and sustainable, and I still lean on what I learned from her. *Graceful Power* is the gift so many of us have been waiting for: the wisdom, clarity and care I was lucky enough to experience one-to-one, now available for every leader who wants to do big work in the world without losing themselves.

Tarana Burke, Founder of the Me Too movement

At a time when leadership advice is cheap and often meaningless, Sally's concept of *Graceful Power* is essential reading for anyone truly committed to developing their leadership capabilities. I've had the privilege of Sally's coaching for 20 years – I would have struggled to survive and succeed without her guidance. It's brilliant she has finally captured what she does in this long overdue book.

Andy Medd, Founder of Mother

Having benefited so much from Sally's coaching myself, I'm delighted that her valuable expertise and thoughtful practical guidance is now available to everyone in this book. I'll be recommending it to other leaders who want to deliver with impact whilst remaining grounded.

Anabel Hoult, Chief Executive Officer at Which?

I found *Graceful Power* a genuinely good read that resonated with my leadership style and philosophy. The line 'you must ground yourself deeply in your humanity' rang absolutely true. In today's highly pressured, fast-moving world, this guide meets leaders at any stage and helps you build a better, more effective version of your leadership-self – to the benefit of your people and teams as much as yourself.

Prof Sir Menelas N Pangalos PhD DSc FRSB FBPhS(Hon) FFPM(Hon) FMedSci FRS, formerly Executive Vice President R&D at AstraZeneca

As someone who has spent decades organizing in the trenches of democracy, I know that lasting change comes not from those who wield power like a weapon, but from those who share it like bread. Sally Netherwood has captured something sacred here – that grace under pressure isn't weakness, it's the kind of strength that moves mountains and transforms hearts. In these times when power is so often abused, this book is both a prophetic call and a practical guide to the leadership our wounded world desperately needs.

LaTosha Brown, Co-Founder of Black Voters Matter Fund and Southern Black Girls & Women

It's a rare skill to be able to not only bring clarity to the complex dynamics of leadership, but to have identified that success actually lies deep within each and every leader. There is no invention required. Sally has brilliantly codified a system for unlocking the *Graceful Power* that lies within all of us. And she's done it in a characteristically Sally way: she's told a story that we can all see ourselves in. This book is bigger than just business – this is a guide for a successful life.

Al MacCuish, Founder and Chairman at Sunshine

After 20 years of working with leaders running an executive search business and having trained to be a coach myself, I have read countless leadership and coaching books. I cannot recommend *Graceful Power* more highly, it offers the most practical guidance for today's challenges. Modern leadership demands adaptability, humanity and the ability to navigate constant change and complexity. It's a tough, often lonely role – and Sally's book gives such insight into successful modern leadership, it feels like having a full-time coach by your side. Practical, accessible and incredibly useful. Thank you, Sally.

Juliet Timms, Founder of Grace Blue Worldwide,
Chair at Grace Blue Europe

Graceful Power is not just a leadership framework; it's a lifeline. Eighteen months after completing my coaching sessions with Sally, I suffered a traumatic brain injury due to Meningoencephalitis and spent a month in Neuro-ICU. The tools I had learned with her became my anchor in the storm – helping me confront my darkest fears, live in congruence, and forge deeper, more meaningful connections with everyone in my life. In a high-pressure leadership role, where I was facing what felt like a certain end, this approach helped me come back not just smarter, but more human. Sally's work is a gift to anyone who wants to lead with strength, authenticity and heart.

Thabang Skwambane, Chief Executive Officer at Nahana Group

Sally is the best leadership coach I have ever had the privilege of working with. By writing this insightful, inspirational and practical guide on *Graceful Power* – complete with clear tools drawn from her years of experience and wisdom working with entrepreneurs, business leaders and game-changers – many more leaders around the world can now learn from her. With Sally as your pocket coaching guide, you can really tap into your own vision, values and purpose as a leader in the 21st century, taking your leadership abilities and influence to the next level with grace, humility and confidence.

Molly Aldridge, Founder and
Chief Executive Officer at The JJ Club Group

As someone who directly benefited from Sally's coaching prior to becoming CEO of the national youth charity OnSide, I can fully vouch for the depth and value of her insight. Sally's wisdom and support helped me step into the authentic leader I wanted to be, clearing away the limiting beliefs that stood in my way. *Graceful Power* beautifully captures the essence of what makes her approach so impactful – a practical and deeply human framework for leading with courage, care and congruence. I have no doubt this book will be an invaluable companion for anyone seeking to lead with impact while staying true to themselves.

Jamie Masraff, Chief Executive Officer at OnSide

Graceful Power offers something genuinely rare: a leadership approach that doesn't ask you to choose between strength and humanity. Drawing on 25 years of coaching experience, it guides you toward the self-awareness that makes leadership feel less like a struggle, because it's harder to lead well when you don't truly know yourself. Whether you're starting your leadership journey or have led for many years, this is a thoughtful companion and practical toolkit for becoming the kind of leader people actually want to follow. In a world that desperately needs more grounded, human leaders, this book is both timely and transformative.

Julia Ingall, Chief People Officer at The Travel Corporation

In defining and exploring what *Graceful Power* means as a leader in the modern world Sally Netherwood has created a truly thought-provoking guide for all leaders. By recognizing at the outset your own individual style and sense of purpose, this book builds on who you are to create a unique, authentic and impactful leadership style. Wherever and whoever you lead, this book will enable you to navigate the complexities of all the many demands the world now places on its leaders and leave you inspired to fulfil your potential.

Lynn Dunne, Partner and Global Board Member at Ashurst LLP

I've recommended Sally to CEOs, celebrities and close friends – and without exception, they all describe her coaching as life-changing. To now have all her wisdom, experience and perspective distilled into an inspiring philosophy and book, accessible to a wider audience, is a true gift to the world.

Carter Murray, formerly Global Chief Executive Officer at FCB

Sally's writing on the persistent paradoxes facing latter day leaders really resonates. Her framing of *Graceful Power* as a way to navigate these challenges is an insightful approach. This book is so worth reading to understand how this can be applicable and addictive to your leadership.

Anna Bateson, Chief Executive Officer at Guardian Media Group

Graceful Power is a wise antidote to the noise of modern leadership. Sally Netherwood shows how courage and care can sit side by side – enabling leaders to act decisively while never losing sight of people. Public servants and business leaders alike will find both clarity and practical guidance here.

Helle Thorning-Schmidt, formerly Prime Minister of Denmark

Graceful Power is the definitive practical playbook for modern leadership. Like any great leader, it does more than just set out the vision. By embracing the contradictions that plague every leader instead of wishing them away and charting a path to harmony by starting from the inside out, it shows us how to become more like the leaders we admire and the leaders we wished we had the opportunity to follow.

Kofi Amoo-Gottfried, Chief Marketing Officer at DoorDash

For the three great loves of my life;
Antony, Noah and Wilkie.

Contents

Part V: Leading with Graceful Power

Introduction

This book is for anyone who wants to lead with greater impact in today's complex and rapidly evolving world. Whether you're an experienced leader or just starting out, whatever your gender, background, field or focus, Graceful Power is for you if you know there's always more to learn, more potential to uncover, a different way of doing things. It's for those who believe that leadership can – and should – be a positive, rewarding experience for both the leader and those they lead.

Graceful Power is for you if you believe leadership isn't about dominance, charm or bravado, but about depth of connection, integrity and calm confidence. It's an invitation to rethink what power looks and feels like when it's at its most effective, sustainable and human.

Over the last 25 years, it's been my joy and privilege to coach a wide range of leaders from around the world – from the most commercially driven organizations to those shaping how we live, work and relate to each other. I've seen these leaders grow more self-assured and clear-sighted, more effective in driving change and influencing behaviour. They become more grounded, consistent and intentional – trustworthy role models in how they live and lead.

A pattern has emerged. As these leaders embrace their inner work, they begin to own their power more fully – steadily, naturally and authentically. They become more effective with less effort. They find the balance between compassionate and commercial leadership, focused on the wellbeing of their people as much as their performance. They learn to lead with both power and grace, and in doing so, experience deeper fulfilment alongside stronger results.

And now, it's your turn.

Through these pages, I'll be the coach in your pocket, encouraging you to do the inner work that shapes your outer impact. This isn't a passive read, but an active partnership. You'll be invited to reflect, practice and try out new ways of thinking and behaving.

Built on tens of thousands of hours of coaching experience, this book demystifies and simplifies leadership development advice. You'll find practical exercises designed to translate insight into action, supporting immediate and sustained growth. As you progress through the chapters, you'll find yourself not only thinking differently about leadership – but leading differently.

We begin by exploring the context: why leaders today need Graceful Power more than ever – the volatile environments they operate in, and the conflicting expectations placed upon them.

In Parts Two, Three and Four, we dive into the practical work. You'll explore the three interwoven qualities that define leaders with Graceful Power: congruence, courage and compassion. Some exercises can be completed as you read, while others may require dedicated focus and time for reflection over a few days or weeks.

Throughout the book, you'll meet stories of leaders who've faced challenges similar to your own. Some are named individuals who have generously agreed to appear in the book. Others are fictionalized composites, drawn from hundreds of coaching conversations over the years.

To support your journey, you'll find:

- Step-by-step guides to each exercise, some with downloadable templates (accessed via the QR code below).
- Two recorded visualizations (also via the QR code), best experienced in a quiet, uninterrupted space.
- Reflective prompts and occasional journalling invitations to deepen your insights.

I recommend using a dedicated notebook for your Graceful Power journey, where you can collect your reflections, ideas and commitments all in one place.

In the final part, we bring everything together. We'll explore how Graceful Power comes to life in your leadership through continued integration and practice, and how this ripples outwards: into your team, your organization, your life, your family, your community and the wider systems you're part of.

I've designed the book so that each part builds on the last, however, you can move through it in whatever way works best for you. Some parts will resonate more than others; some exercises will stretch you further than others. I hope you'll find what you were looking for when you picked up this book, and a whole lot more besides.

Wherever you begin this journey, I wish you a rewarding experience as you expand your own Graceful Power.

PART I

UNDERSTANDING GRACEFUL POWER

Chapter 1

What is Graceful Power?

There are moments when leadership transcends authority and becomes something infinitely more powerful.

On a February morning in 1990, Nelson Mandela walked slowly through the prison gates. After 27 years of confinement, he smiled, lifted his hand, and spoke not of anger, but of peace and freedom. He chose reconciliation over revenge, inviting a divided nation to heal.

Twenty-five years later, in a quiet church in Charleston, Barack Obama stood at the pulpit, honouring the lives taken in a brutal act of hate. When he paused mid-eulogy and began to sing Amazing Grace, he transformed grief into a shared moment of hope.

As fear rippled across the world in 2020, Jacinda Ardern appeared on a self-filmed livestream from her living room, wearing a comfy sweatshirt. She spoke candidly, with warmth and clarity. Connecting and reassuring a nation that they would face the COVID-19 crisis together.

Each of these moments carried the same essence: Graceful Power – leadership rooted in composure, courage and human connection.

When I first began sharing the idea of this book, people's reactions to the paradoxical concept of Graceful Power, were fascinating. Many leaders immediately recognized it. They said it captured the type of leadership they admired and aspired to. A few, however, jumped to the conclusion that this must be a leadership book for women.

Perhaps that reaction comes from a familiar pattern: books written by men are assumed to be for everyone, while books written by women are often considered more niche or gendered, even when the ideas are universal. But sometimes this reaction stems from something deeper – an ingrained belief that men cannot lead with grace, or that women should cultivate a "softer" version of power.

Graceful Power is *not* a softening of leadership; it's a strengthening. It is *not* a feminine trait, but a universal leadership strength that is needed today more than ever. It allows leaders to act with clarity, courage and composure in the face of complexity and pressure – the way Mandela, Obama and Ardern did in those defining moments.

Everything I've learnt in 25 years of coaching leaders around the world proves this to be true.

The leadership goals of my clients are remarkably consistent across gender, industry and geography. They want to lead with greater clarity and confidence; to get the best from themselves, their teams and organizations; to meet the demands of their role without burning out and to feel proud of who they are becoming and the impact they are having along the way.

I've worked with men and women who needed to bring more power to their leadership – more assertiveness, boundary-setting and willingness to challenge. I've also worked with both women and men who needed to bring more grace – more authenticity, empathy and care.

As our work together progresses, and their self-understanding deepens, they begin to lead with more ease and more impact. Their leadership expands. They trust themselves more. They reconnect with their values and their vision. They stop wasting energy on inner battles and start channelling it outwards, to where it really makes a difference. This is what it means to lead with Graceful Power. Not a "soft" alternative to traditional leadership, but a far more effective and sustainable form of it.

We notice Graceful Power in those leaders who take bold action with apparent ease. Who calmly and intentionally stand by their words, honouring their values even when it's uncomfortable, unexpected or unusual. These leaders have learnt to balance the conflicting demands of modern leadership in a way that feels both natural and deeply human. Taking care of themselves, their business and their people – who feel as valued as the results they deliver.

Everyone, including you, can bring more Graceful Power to their leadership if they choose to. It requires some time, attention and practice as you steadily iterate and improve your approach, but you will get there. Whether you simply need to refine a few aspects of your current leadership or take on a more thorough transformation, this book will guide you.

Case study: Allan Barton – bringing grace to his power

Let me share Allan Barton's leadership story – a story that exemplifies a transition to Graceful Power.

Allan was a shy, sensitive boy – dyslexic at a time when there was little understanding or appreciation for the unique strengths this way of thinking can bring. Labelled early as "unlikely to go far", he followed his father's advice and joined a national electricity supplier – a steady job, with steady prospects.

Once in the workplace, Allan's natural problem-solving ability and project management skills began to shine. Determined and task-focused, he developed a reputation for tenacity. With a bashful smile, Allan now describes his early leadership style as that of a "honey badger".

This wasn't a metaphor I'd heard before. Allan explained that honey badgers are among the most ferocious animals in the world. Roughly the size of a spaniel, they're unafraid to take on lions. In Allan's words: "They don't take prisoners while getting the job done – even if it means attacking the lion."

In practice, this meant Allan led with a laser-like focus on delivery. He interrogated every detail, constantly questioning his team. He became a master micromanager – tracking every action with exhaustive spreadsheets. Looking back, Allan is candid: "I didn't trust them.

I thought they'd get it wrong, spend too much, or miss the deadline." Anyone who failed to deliver was met with his full frustration – unfiltered and unrelenting.

This strategy appeared to work. Projects were delivered on time and on budget. Allan was rewarded with promotions and rising pay. On paper, he was succeeding, but the personal cost was mounting. He was working six days a week, carrying the full burden of performance on his own shoulders. His health suffered. He became distant from his family. He was climbing the ladder – but felt drained, disconnected and deeply unfulfilled.

What makes Allan's story extraordinary is what happened next.

Now a company director, Allan was invited to take part in a 360° feedback process as part of his organization's investment in leadership development. It was the first time he'd received formal feedback from his team, and it floored him.

"They hated me", he says simply – the sting of that realization still sharp years later.

His first instinct, true to form, was pure honey badger: "Fire them all!" But thankfully, the wiser part of Allan held him back. He paused, reflected and began to genuinely consider what he'd heard.

Gradually, Allan came to appreciate that it wasn't that his team hated him. It was that they felt unseen, unheard and untrusted.

With courage and humility, Allan chose to evolve his leadership. He began asking more questions, inviting his team into decisions, and listening – really listening – to how they felt about their work. As he extended more compassion to them, he found himself becoming more compassionate toward himself too.

What's striking, meeting Allan today, is how deeply attuned he is to the needs and feelings of others – but in those earlier years, he was living a life that denied this part of himself. His early leadership style, while effective on the surface, was out of step with who he really was.

To his relief, performance didn't suffer. In fact, it improved. When Allan later announced he was leaving the company, some of the same team members who had once criticized him now expressed sincere regret at his departure.

Allan didn't stop there. He made leadership growth a lifelong priority. He devoured books, attended courses, sought out mentors. He adopted a new mantra: "You're only as good as the team you lead." He focused on developing his people, understanding their perspectives and connecting them to a shared purpose.

One particularly powerful example came in a later role, when Allan led the transformation of waste and recycling services for north-east London. With his senior team, he co-created a bold new vision and a shared set of values and behaviours. At the heart of it: a clear and compelling purpose – to provide a life-enriching experience for everyone involved.

This wasn't merely a slogan. Employees were consulted, engaged and made to feel genuinely valued. Some tough decisions were made about those unwilling to adapt – but Allan and his team held firm in their commitment to the culture.

Performance followed and targets were met or exceeded. Yet, for Allan, it was a quiet moment of feedback that meant the most.

At a celebratory team evening at the Walthamstow greyhound track, a large, stern-looking waste handler approached Allan. He braced himself for criticism. Instead, the man simply said: "I want to thank you for this evening. I've worked for the council for 15 years, and this is the first time anyone has ever said thank you to me."

Allan Barton's journey illustrates the transformative potential of Graceful Power. His early success was built on control and determination. But it was only when he embraced congruence (aligning his leadership with his true, empathetic self), courage (facing uncomfortable truths and being willing to change) and compassion (building genuine care and trust in his teams) that his leadership and wellbeing truly flourished.

In the chapters ahead, we'll explore how Graceful Power emerges through these three interwoven qualities: congruence, courage and compassion. You'll find practical exercises, simple frameworks and reflections to help you recognize these qualities in yourself, and strengthen them so they become a natural, reliable part of how you lead. Along the way, you'll meet more leaders who have walked this path with the courage to face their limitations and grow. By the end, you'll be ready to lead with a Graceful Power that is unmistakably your own.

In the next chapter, let's take a closer look at the paradoxical expectations of leaders today, which make Graceful Power so vital.

Chapter 2

The paradox of modern leadership

It's 8:15 am, and you're already running late. Your phone is buzzing relentlessly with notifications – each one demanding immediate attention. Overnight, three emails arrived from a challenging colleague, expecting urgent responses. Your team is anxiously waiting for you to clarify strategy changes from yesterday's senior leadership meeting. Meanwhile, news alerts about a critical cybersecurity breach in your industry flash across your screen. Before your first coffee, the day's pressures are stacking up, pulling you in every direction at once.

Welcome to modern leadership: a role defined not just by complexity, but by paradox.

Leading people has never been easy – getting others to do what's needed, ideally with some level of enthusiasm, while being held personally accountable for the outcome of their endeavour is inherently challenging. But today, leaders are pulled between seemingly opposing, but similarly important priorities on a daily basis. The tension this creates is more intense and contradictory than ever before.

We expect leaders to be confident, decisive and directive – able to steer the ship firmly through storms. At the same time, we want them to be emotionally intelligent, inclusive and responsive – creating safe environments where everyone feels heard and valued. We want leaders who set uncompromising standards, but who welcome candid feedback and admit their mistakes freely. They must lead boldly from the front, yet stay humble, approachable and deeply human. To lead today means continuously being stretched between competing truths.

This isn't merely challenging; it's exhausting. It's no surprise that even highly capable leaders often wonder if they're enough. If they are up to the task. If they even *want* to be up to it.

The inter-connectivity of business and communication has opened up the world in many positive ways, offering access to new customers and a broader talent pool; the opportunity to reduce costs through global sourcing and to spread risk through diversified markets; facilitating the exchange of ideas and knowledge to drive innovation and best practice. However, as well as opportunity, globalization brings complexity. When things go wrong, they can go wrong globally.

Consider what unfolded on Friday 19 July, 2024. News alerts came flooding in, detailing the most significant global IT outage ever recorded. Within hours, American Airlines had grounded every flight. Poland's largest container terminal stopped functioning. New Zealand's parliament lost access to vital data. In the UK, doctors' surgeries and pharmacies couldn't access patient records, while elective surgeries in Germany were cancelled. Banks, supermarkets and media outlets went dark. All from a single faulty update pushed by cybersecurity firm CrowdStrike, shutting down 8.5 million Windows systems worldwide, affecting many millions of lives.

As I watched these chaotic events unfold, my thoughts turned immediately to the thousands of leaders forced into rapid response mode – without warning and through no fault of their own. Each had to simultaneously appear confident, decisive and reassuring, while internally navigating confusion and uncertainty. They needed quick, firm decisions to restore systems, but also deep empathy for employees, customers, passengers and patients affected by the crisis. Once the dust settled, they knew that each decision would be closely scrutinized by boards, regulators and the public.

Modern leadership isn't only pressured during crises. Today, leaders operate under a relentless microscope every day. Online platforms intended to boost transparency have also created constant accountability. Leaders' daily behaviours, decisions and attitudes are now publicly reviewed – anonymously and permanently – on sites like Glassdoor. Not long ago, the idea of a CEO being publicly rated by their employees would have seemed absurd. Now, it's expected. Leadership success is no longer measured solely by results, but by values, character and cultural impact. Society expects our leaders not just to deliver, but to be a force for good.

Even the process of selecting leaders has shifted dramatically. Previously, recruiters focused primarily on experience and technical qualifications. Today, organizations brief recruiters on the desired culture, future vision, anticipated challenges and opportunities. Headhunters must now identify leaders with influencing skills, adaptability, emotional intelligence and the capacity to galvanize experts rather than simply being the expert themselves. This shift fundamentally alters how leaders must view their role and how they develop themselves for advancement.

Amid this complexity, leaders face a relentless barrage of conflicting demands:

- They must deliver results today – hit targets, manage crises and protect the bottom line – while simultaneously investing in innovation, nurturing talent and securing long-term futures. Lean too much toward immediate results, and future viability suffers. Focus too heavily on the future, and today's results falter.
- Leaders must act decisively, swiftly making tough calls under pressure. Yet, they must also foster inclusive environments, welcoming diverse voices and careful deliberation. Move too fast, you risk alienating your team; move too slowly, you risk losing critical momentum.
- They must show strength, confidence and authority. Yet simultaneously, they must openly acknowledge mistakes, show vulnerability and empathize genuinely. Project too much strength, and you're seen as arrogant. Show too much vulnerability, and you're perceived as weak.

- Leaders must also navigate the paradox of meeting commercial objectives while genuinely caring for their people. Delivering profits and shareholder value is non-negotiable, but equally vital is creating conditions where employees feel valued, respected and inspired. Push too hard for financial performance, and morale suffers; prioritize wellbeing without performance, and commercial success diminishes.
- The role demands constant availability and extraordinary commitment – often glorifying burnout as proof of dedication. Yet sustained high performance requires self-care, healthy boundaries and personal wellbeing.
- Leaders are inundated with data, dashboards and expert advice, yet the heart of effective leadership is clarity, prioritization and simplicity. Critical tasks – reflection, deep thinking, trust-building – remain mostly invisible and undervalued, while visible missteps are amplified.

Each of these paradoxes represents essential yet opposing truths. Both sides are correct. And leaders are expected to hold them all, all of the time.

As I write this book, the pace of change continues to accelerate dramatically. In just the few months between delivering the manuscript and its publication, geopolitics, technology and social expectations will have shifted again, possibly profoundly.

To thrive in this turbulent landscape, you will need to embrace the tension between these paradoxical demands. You'll build your agility to respond to immediate pressures while maintaining clarity around your long-term vision. You'll navigate uncertainty confidently, taking bold decisions despite ambiguity, doubt and risk.

Above all, you must ground yourself deeply in your humanity. In an increasingly automated and artificially intelligent world, a leader's human relationships will become their greatest strength. You'll need to lean fully into those interactions you find challenging, tackling the conversations and situations which make you feel uncomfortable or vulnerable. And you'll need to take great care of yourself and your team, not simply to avoid burnout whilst constantly challenging people to develop and grow, but to actively create conditions where people flourish and organizational objectives are achieved.

To do this, you'll need to move beyond merely managing paradox. You'll need to solve it. You'll need Graceful Power – and this book will be your guide. Graceful Power isn't about having all the answers. It's about consciously and confidently navigating all the demands and expectations, making thoughtful choices, and using your presence to create clarity amid complexity.

Chapter 3

The qualities of Graceful Power

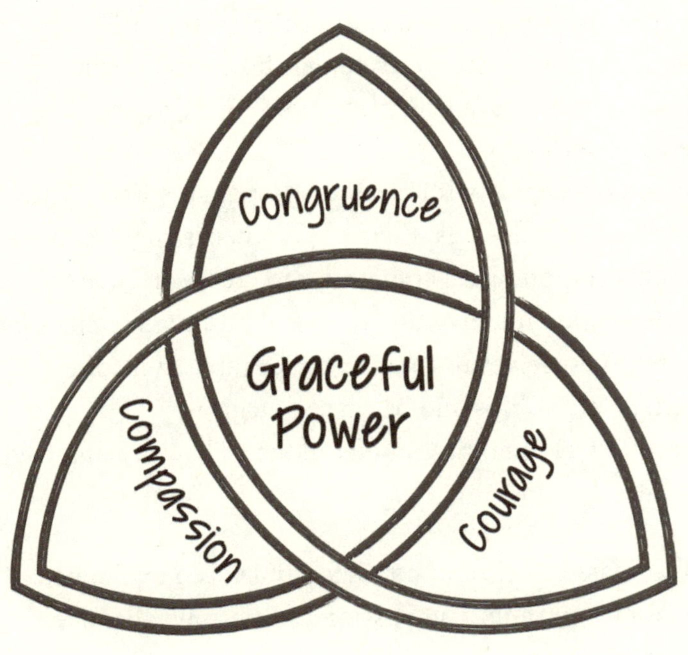

Graceful Power flows from three deeply human qualities that are constantly working together: congruence, courage and compassion. These aren't lofty ideals or fixed personality traits – they are consciously chosen behaviours. Each can be cultivated and strengthened through intentional practice. They're a mix of mindset and skillset – the way you think and feel on the inside, and the way you act on the outside.

Congruence is about personal alignment and reliability in what you think and feel, say and do. It starts with knowing yourself – what you value and aspire to, your particular strengths and what you want to stand for. Then you bring that clarity into your actions, decisions and behaviour. People can sense this integrity. They trust you not because you're always right, but because you're real and consistent.

Courage is the willingness to take the necessary action even when things are uncertain or uncomfortable. It's holding your ground when it would be easier to step back, making the tough calls, having the difficult conversations, and speaking the truth with care. It's about acknowledging your fears, your vulnerability and daring to move forward even when the path isn't clear, holding steady so that others can hold their nerve too.

Compassion begins with a genuine openness and curiosity about other people – their feelings, their hopes, their struggles. It's the ability to listen fully, respond with empathy, and create an environment where everyone feels individually valued, useful and competent – motivated to bring their best selves to their work. Compassion softens resistance, strengthens relationships and helps people grow.

None of these qualities stands alone. They are intertwined and interdependent.

- Compassion without courage can lead to avoidance.
- Courage without compassion can become abrasive.
- Congruence without either can become rigid or remote.

Together, they form a robust foundation – one that is both firm and adaptable, both strong and human.

These three qualities work in dynamic balance – regulating, reinforcing and refining one another. They create the kind of confident authority that doesn't demand attention but earns it. That steadies others and inspires them. That makes space for complexity and paradox without being consumed by them.

Graceful Power is not about changing who you are. It's about becoming even more fully yourself – and using that self as a powerful, conscious force for good.

Creating the conditions for your growth

Every reader of this book, just like every leader who's been my client, starts their journey to Graceful Power from a different place. You may need to focus on one of the three interwoven qualities in particular – perhaps compassion is a blind spot, or congruence. Or you may need to improve the intentionality with which you weave all three of the qualities throughout your leadership.

Wherever you are beginning your journey, aim to adopt the open, curious attitude of a learner as you work through the coming chapters. No matter how experienced or accomplished – there is always a fresh insight to be gained, a new technique to learn or a new perspective to propel you further along the path of Graceful Power.

I've learnt so much in bringing this book together – both from the people I've interviewed and the books I've read. But most significantly of all, from the time I've carved out to reflect on all I've learnt from my clients and our leadership conversations over the years.

Creating the time for reflection is possibly the most undervalued leadership activity. This is understandable as it is invisible work – usually done alone and often, through necessity, carried out away from the workplace to avoid interruption. Yet, it is so vital. It is particularly important to developing and honing your Graceful Power.

Throughout the coming pages you will find regular suggestions to reflect on your leadership – sometimes alongside an exercise, sometimes in response to a concept you've been reading about. Please embrace these opportunities – carve out the quiet time away from distractions. Jot down your thoughts, scribble a list of ideas and actions or simply have a good think as you walk through the park.

My intention is for you to feel inspired to evolve and expand your whole approach to leading. I've put all I can into this book, now it's over to you. Only you can choose to deepen, embed and bring to life any insights you may glean.

PART II

CONGRUENCE

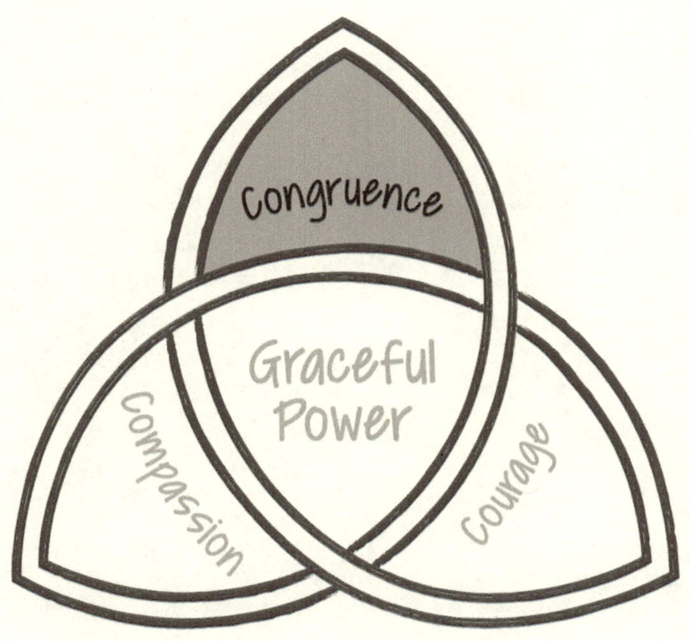

In this part of the book, we'll explore how congruence builds the foundation for your Graceful Power:

- Chapter 4 – *The role of congruence in Graceful Power*. We'll examine what congruent leadership looks like in practice, the qualities it draws on and the powerful impact it creates.
- Chapter 5 – *Deepening self-awareness*. Here, you'll develop a richer understanding of yourself as a leader. Through practical tools you'll create a personal framework that guides your choices and strengthens your integrity.
- Chapter 6 – *Developing authentic agility*. Finally, we'll focus on applying your self-awareness in the messy, dynamic reality of leadership. You'll learn how to build emotional mastery, lead with clarity and intention, and keep evolving through a mindset of continuous improvement.

By the end of this section, you'll have a clear sense of what drives you, steadies you and shapes your unique leadership style. Congruence gives you the solid ground from which your courage and compassion can flourish – and where your Graceful Power begins to take root.

Chapter 4

The role of congruence in Graceful Power

A few years ago, Helena came to me for coaching on her leadership approach. She'd been deeply moved by the tributes to her late father-in-law at his funeral. He had lived a rich life, holding leadership roles in business, the community and a variety of cultural and sporting organizations.

The speakers leading the tributes spoke of how well liked, respected and trusted he was. What stood out most for Helena was how consistently he showed up – no matter where he was or who he was with. Whether you met him at work, in a voluntary role or at a social event, he would be unmistakably true to himself.

Helena was struck by the contrast with her own experience. "That's not me", she admitted. "I'm a completely different person at work than I am at home or with my friends – and it's exhausting. I've developed an act that gets me by professionally, but it doesn't feel true. I just don't know how to lead any other way."

It was clear, hearing Helena describe him and his influence on others, that her father-in-law was a man with Graceful Power – reliably true to himself, bold when facing a challenge and deeply caring in how he related to others. The congruence of his leadership left a legacy that inspired Helena to take stock of her own.

She recognized the toll that leading reactively or in the way she thought she "should" was having on her. How much harder and less fulfilling it was to *act* like a leader than to simply *be* herself as a leader.

Together, we explored the whole of Helena's life: what mattered to her, what gave her energy and what drained her. We uncovered the beliefs she lived by and the dreams she had for her future. Slowly, she began to evolve her thinking, identifying outdated habits and creating a new blueprint for how she wanted to live and lead.

With that clarity, everything became easier. She had a framework for guiding her decisions, handling demands and staying centred while responding flexibly to what the moment required. Once she gave herself permission to bring more of herself forward, she found she could lead with far more ease, and far greater impact.

What does congruent leadership look like?

In the context of Graceful Power, congruent leadership means alignment – between values and behaviour, intention and impact, inner beliefs and outward actions. Leaders who show congruence earn trust. Their presence feels steady, coherent and real. Their actions make sense because they are grounded in a strong sense of self.

Congruence doesn't happen by accident. Gracefully powerful leaders do the inner work. They lead with intention and shape their impact *on purpose*. The rewards of this effort are twofold:

1. It's easier and far more fulfilling to be this leader.
2. It's easier and far more fulfilling to follow this leader.

There's a saying, attributed to the leader Mahatma Gandhi, that, "Happiness is when what you think, what you say and what you do are in harmony."

Bring that harmony to your leadership, and not only will you feel more fulfilled, but you'll also enrich the lives of the people around you.

When your values, words and actions align, people trust you. A working environment built on trust supports and encourages people to do their best work. This is not about being perfect. It's about being real and consistent. When people trust their leader, they speak up more. They bring their ideas. They step up to challenges and go the extra mile.

Congruent leadership creates a stable, grounded atmosphere where people feel safe to contribute, to collaborate and to grow. Over time, this creates a high-performing culture that is powered by trust, rather than driven by pressure.

Revealing your true self

The greatest joy in my work is helping someone uncover the hidden potential that lies beneath layers of unconscious habits, outdated beliefs or long-practised behaviours that no longer serve them. Developing Graceful Power isn't about changing who you are – it's about revealing your true self and allowing it to shine.

This starts with exploration: discovering or reaffirming what really matters to you: your values, your aspirations, your unique leadership style and your sense of purpose. As you work through the exercises in this section and build reflective practice into your routine, you'll find that living and leading congruently becomes more natural, more energizing and more rewarding.

Together, we'll create a uniquely personal framework that equips you to take your place in the world with elegance, clarity and confidence.

Leadership transitions

Transitions into leadership – or into greater responsibility – are often seen as a time to shift focus. A time to change ourselves to fit the role. To dim the light on personal values in service of collective success. To become more steely in outlook, more results-focused to build that high-performance team.

In reality, leadership progression calls for the opposite: making time to build a deeper connection with who you are and what you believe. Building alignment with your role and organizational culture and purpose. Graceful Power demands a clear-eyed understanding of what's right and wrong for you, what you stand for and what you don't. It asks you to notice what energizes you and what drains you, what makes you feel purposeful, valued and valuable.

If you want to build a team of highly motivated individuals working toward a shared goal, you'll need them to have that same connection with themselves too. That's how you harness energy and commitment to work towards a unified mission.

The yearning to be seen

We know from countless workplace studies that people yearn to be recognized for who they are, not just what they deliver. Gallup and Workhuman's[1] longitudinal recognition study, which tracked 3,500 employees over two years, showed that high-quality recognition – valuing identity as well as contribution – dramatically reduced turnover and job-hunting. Recent research published in *Nature*[2] found that a sense of belonging, where individuals feel genuinely valued for their authentic selves, directly boosts motivation and retention.

In this age of accelerating advances in artificial intelligence, the leaders who truly value the being of humans will become ever more influential, beguiling and needed. Congruent leaders meet this yearning. Because they know who they are, they can hold space for others to be themselves too. Because they manage themselves well, they can lead with curiosity, not control. And because their leadership is rooted in authenticity, they naturally create workplaces that invite authenticity in return.

By giving yourself permission to more fully express yourself, you will give others permission to do the same. This is how congruence becomes more than personal integrity – it becomes powerfully influential.

The responsibility to be known

The desire to be understood is deeply human. Yet the responsibility for being seen doesn't rest solely with others. It's tempting to wait – for your boss, your colleague, your partner – to ask the right questions and uncover your values, dreams and aspirations.

But if someone asked you today, could you give them a clear answer? Could you describe what matters to you, how you make decisions, what fuels you – in a way that helps them understand how best to work with you, lead you or love you?

Don't worry if you can't – most people find this challenging. It takes time and attention to work it out. Yet when you do, it is powerful and liberating. To truly value the humanity of others, we must first turn inward. No matter how well you think you know yourself, there's always another layer to peel away, another insight to discover.

Leaders with Graceful Power use this self-awareness to cultivate self-possession: the ability to move through the world with calm confidence, grace under pressure and purposeful impact.

Qualities of congruent leaders

Leaders who demonstrate congruence strike a powerful balance between dependable authenticity – which builds trust, and agile flexibility – which enables them to respond to an ever-changing world.

This balance is not easy to achieve. Navigating the tension between being reliably consistent and reliably adaptable calls for high emotional intelligence: deep self-awareness combined with strong self-management. Congruent leaders are anchored in what they believe and what they stand for. That anchoring allows them to adapt without losing themselves. They:

- live by their core values;
- envision the leader they are becoming;
- connect to a personal sense of purpose; and
- aspire to leadership behaviours that expand their impact and influence.

With this self-awareness, they lead with intent. They:

- regulate their emotions and express them constructively;
- take responsibility for their impact and lead by example;
- reflect on their own behaviour before responding to the behaviour of others;
- acknowledge their strengths and weaknesses while staying open to learning and improvement; and
- align personal and organizational values, shaping culture from within.

Finding congruence isn't a one-time achievement. It is a lifelong, iterative process. The person we are in our twenties will have evolved by our forties, and again in our sixties and eighties. As life unfolds, it enriches our understanding of ourselves and the world. Our ups and downs, triumphs and tragedies, all deepen our wisdom and continually inform how we lead.

Gauging your self-awareness

So, how do you gauge your level of self-awareness and whether it needs work? What does a deeply self-aware leader know that a moderately self-aware one doesn't?

I have an unscientific but practical assessment that I sometimes use when I meet a potential client for the first time. It helps me understand what level of self-awareness we are starting from. I might ask some questions directly, but mostly I'm listening for evidence of an ability to clearly articulate what is important to them and how they feel about things.

Try it for yourself now. Imagine I'm sitting across from you and asking these questions. I'm asking with genuine curiosity to know you, without any judgement. How confidently could you answer?

1. What are the core values that guide your life and leadership?
2. What kind of person and leader do you hope to become?
3. What's it all for? What legacy do you hope to leave behind?

4. When things get tough, how do you re-centre yourself, recharge your motivation and boost your resilience?
5. What situations or environments tend to trigger an unhelpful response in you? How does this impact your leadership?
6. How are you feeling right now? Name the specific emotions you are experiencing.
7. When you are performing at your leadership best, what are you doing? What behaviours or activities are you pursuing?
8. What are your areas of weakness as a leader? What do you shy away from or avoid?
9. If I were to ask your team and colleagues about your leadership strengths and weaknesses, would they say the same as you?

A strongly self-aware leader will know the answers to most or all of these questions and, in the right circumstances, be able to share them clearly, calmly and honestly. Not to impress anyone or to defend themselves, but simply to share their understanding of themselves and what makes them tick. This self-knowledge allows them to lead themselves better and therefore lead others better too.

Creating your Code of Congruence

Whether your answers to the earlier questions came easily or felt more tentative, the next chapter will help you go deeper. Through case studies, practical exercises and tips, you'll be gathering the raw material for something powerful: your Code of Congruence.

Think of it as a living framework that captures your values, aspirations, good habits and ambitions. A reliable reminder of how you want to live and lead. It offers a firm foundation of authenticity on which your Graceful Power can grow.

You'll find a blank template in the Appendix or via the QR code shared in the Introduction. The intention is for you to bring all the insights from the coming exercises onto a single page, which you can revisit and update as your leadership evolves:

- to keep you grounded when things feel confusing;
- to steer decisions for yourself, your team and your organization; and
- to remind you of the kind of leader you're choosing to become.

The exercises that feed directly into your Code of Congruence are:

- Honouring your values;
- Visualizing your Future Self;
- Crafting your Leadership Signature; and
- Clarifying your purpose.

You might want to jot notes in a journal as you work through each exercise, then capture the headline insights in your Code. Or you might prefer to adapt the template so it works in a way that feels most natural to you. What matters is that you create something you can return to again and again – a personal compass for leading with congruence.

Chapter 5

Deepening self-awareness

In the last chapter, we began to explore the importance of congruence – how it can make it easier to lead with greater influence, and how it can make your leadership easier to follow as people come to trust you more, confident in your consistency when responding to events and making decisions. Now it's time to translate that understanding into practice.

This chapter is designed to be highly experiential. I'll guide you through a series of exercises to deepen your self-awareness.

We'll begin by defining your values – the core essence of you. From there, we'll look ahead to your Future Self and the kind of leader you aspire to be. Later, we'll clarify your sense of purpose and connect it to the impact you want to have, before considering the everyday leadership behaviours that will help you stay aligned and effective.

I recommend approaching each exercise individually, rather than trying to tackle the whole chapter in one sitting. Set aside an hour of uninterrupted time for each, noting down the insights you uncover. Expect these insights to deepen over the following days and weeks as you reflect further, put your learning into practice and layer on your findings from the other exercises. Gift yourself the richness of time to explore and reflect, learn and grow – capturing and refining the key points in your Code of Congruence as you go, shaping it into a uniquely personal and meaningful document.

Just as your leadership will evolve, your Code of Congruence will evolve too. You'll return to it throughout this book and beyond, adding depth as you continue to learn more about yourself – such as emotional mastery in the next chapter, and the courageous practices that follow. Think of it as the living framework of your Graceful Power: a structure you'll keep strengthening and shaping as you grow.

HONOURING YOUR VALUES

Your values are the principles of living that truly matter to you. They are the essence of what makes you "you" – sometimes subtly and sometimes profoundly different from everyone else. Values are not aspirations or a moral code. They don't reflect who you *should* be; they reflect who you *love* being. They form your inner compass, shaping how you feel about your life and the world around you. They let you know when you're on course and when you're not.

Imagine driving along a smooth, well-signposted road. Your sat-nav is calmly guiding you, your favourite music is playing and the journey feels effortless. You arrive feeling relaxed and content, having enjoyed the ride.

Now imagine the same journey, but the road is cracked and full of potholes. Your sat-nav freezes and you're left navigating by guesswork, reacting anxiously to the unpredictable conditions. You arrive feeling frazzled, tense and far from your best self.

Living in alignment with your values is like travelling that first road. There's a sense of harmony, of being in tune with yourself. When your values are not honoured – by others or by yourself – you feel unsettled and off-track. The journey may continue, but it feels joyless and stressful.

One of the secrets to a fulfilling life, and the foundation for leading congruently, is to consciously honour your values. When you connect with your most significant values, it's like receiving a map for the best route – the one that gives you the smoothest, most meaningful ride.

When our values are dishonoured, it is uncomfortable. We can tolerate that discomfort briefly – and sometimes we have to – but prolonged misalignment drains us. We may feel resentful or even victimized. When you understand which of your values are being challenged in a particular situation it brings greater clarity, allowing you to tolerate the discomfort as you make decisions to restore your integrity.

Take my client, Franklyn, a CEO who was often infuriated by two investors on his board. He saw them as self-serving and duplicitous, which left him feeling hostile and on edge. As a result of this strong emotional discomfort, Franklyn avoided engaging with these two investors whenever he could. His emotional energy was being drained by the tension. When we looked at the situation through the lens of his values, it became clear: the investors' behaviour in board meetings clashed with two of Franklyn's core values – open, honest collaboration and collective success.

Worse than that: Franklyn's own response – withdrawing and becoming adversarial – was pulling him even further out of alignment and causing him to neglect some of his responsibility as CEO. Recognizing this, he made a deliberate choice to lead with his values, even in interactions where they felt most under threat. He reached out to those investors, sought to understand them better and shared his own goals and principles. The relationship didn't become warm, but it became productive, respectful and far less emotionally taxing for Franklyn.

So, does knowing your values make the road of life magically smooth? Not quite, but it gives you the information you need to navigate with greater ease and clarity.

Your values may be expressed differently in different settings, but their essence remains. Choosing to honour your values, even when it's difficult and you are being challenged, is a powerful act. The discomfort of doing so will pass; the integrity you gain will last.

Exercise: Identifying your values

This exercise helps you build that personal map. The aim is to articulate 8–10 values that resonate deeply within you. To do this, you are going to recall experiences that either honoured or dishonoured your values and reconnect with how this felt.

This process will take a little time, perhaps over a few days, with a mix of focused reflection and unhurried mulling. You may be tempted to speed up the process by picking values from a list but this alone can result in an intellectual exercise and rather sterile value definitions. It's much better to get out of your head and connect with your heart and body, too.

- Don't aim for tidy, single-word values. Be creative with short phrases or metaphors that really mean something to you.
- Don't aim for perfection. Your values list will be a living document you continue to refine.
- Do notice how it feels in your body when you are connected to an important value. It's often described as a sense of "rightness" – calm and clear.
- Do be honest with yourself. This list is only for you. Ignore the internal voice telling you what "should" matter, or what used to matter. Focus on what is true for you *today*, when you feel most yourself.

Some examples of core values from clients:

- *Life is an adventure* – embrace every moment.
- *Mountain ski guide* – get them ready and let them run.
- *Building a solid crew* – who love to work together and win together.
- *Count on me* – trustworthy and reliable.
- *Getting noticed* – standing out from the crowd.
- *Back on my feet fast* – setbacks happen; it's how fast I bounce back that matters.

Notice how unique and personal these values are? No dictionary definitions here, just statements that bring clarity and a sense of rightness to each individual leader. Here are three of my own:

- *Wild white horse* – alive, unrestrained, free.
- *Mastery and accomplishment* – if it's worth doing, it's worth doing well.
- *Commitment is 100%* – if I say I'll do something, I will.

Do I always live up to them? I wish! But they stir something deep within me. They bring me back to myself in moments of conflict, doubt or stress. They help me make better choices and stay on track, fully myself.

So, get creative. Pick up a pencil and a blank page, and allow yourself to start messy. Scrawl your thoughts and insights as they appear, then gradually shape them into a list of values. If you find yourself really stuck and need inspiration, you can download a long list of values via the QR code in the Introduction – but try exploring what emerges when you engage your imagination and emotions first.

Ten prompts to discover your values

Here are some prompts to spark your exploration. Take your time with each, some will be more fruitful than others, but give each one a chance to reveal something valuable. Look out for repetition or themes that link your experiences together.

1. Remember one or two of your favourite ever holidays. What made them so enjoyable, so special? What kind of person did you get to be?
2. Reflect on a high point of your working life. What made it energizing? What environment, behaviours and beliefs brought out the best in you?
3. Now recall a low point at work. What made it so difficult? What was missing?
4. Who is the most aggravating person you know? What exactly bothers you? What do they do or say that you find so challenging?
5. What do your family and friends completely rely on you for?
6. What do people tease you about? What does that reveal?
7. What animals are you drawn to and why? What do they represent for you?
8. What's been keeping you up at night? What does that reveal about your priorities?

9. Which public figures do you admire and feel an affinity with? What behaviours or principles do they demonstrate that resonate strongly with you?
10. When were you last angry and what about? What behaviours or attitudes were evident that felt so wrong to you? What was missing?

Now, taking all the time you need, draw your notes together to create a list of what is most important to you. A list of values, that when honoured make life feel good, right and clear to you.

Exercise: Intentional value honouring

Let's look at how you can use your list of values to turn insights into action. By ranking, rating and reflecting on how well you're honouring your values in daily life, you'll build a stronger connection between what matters most to you and how you show up in the world. The goal is to bring greater awareness to your behaviour which will support you in making conscious choices that reinforce your sense of congruence – especially in moments that test it.

1. Rank

Begin by ordering your values in terms of importance. Which ones most truly define who you are and how you want to live? Cull your list to no more than 8–10 to keep it manageable. If some values feel closely linked, see if they can be grouped under a broader heading. If you feel torn, try using one of your values as a guide to help you make the decision.

2. Rate

Take a look at how well you're currently living each value. Using a scale from 1–10, rate how fully you're honouring each one in your personal life and again in your work life. Be honest with yourself, this is about noticing where you are getting it right and where more attention is needed.

Draw out the table below (or download via the QR code in the Introduction) so that you can easily view all the scores together for comparison. My values and scores are included here to give you the idea.

Value	Personal life	Work life
1. Wild White Horse	8	8
2. Mastery + Accomplishment	7	9
3. Commitment is 100%	7	7
4.		
5.		
6.		
7.		
8.		
9.		
10.		

3. Review

Now take a step back and look at your scores. What patterns or anomalies jump out? Are there values that are strong in one domain of life but not the other? Which ones are currently being honoured well? Which ones are being neglected? What fresh insights does this reveal?

4. Reflect

Choose two or three values that, if lived more fully over the next week, would create the biggest positive shift in how you feel and how you lead. What would change if you gave these particular values more space and more weight in your decisions and actions over the next seven days?

5. Revere

Hold your chosen values with intention and respect. Keep them front-of-mind over the next week with alerts on your phone or sticky notes on your desk. After each meeting or conversation – or as you tidy up at the end of the day – pause to ask yourself:

- How well did I honour my chosen values?
- Where did I compromise them?
- What can I learn from this?
- What will I do differently next time?

6. Revisit

When the week has passed, return to your full list. Re-rate your values and notice what's changed. Has your sense of alignment improved? Choose your next values for focus and continue this cycle of intentional value honouring. Congruence is not about getting it right once – it's a way of living that deepens over time.

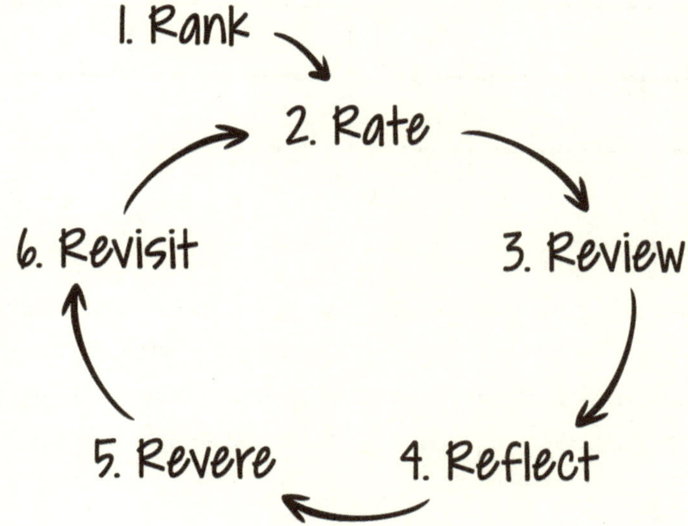

Now write your values, in order of importance, into your Code of Congruence.

A note on anger and values

Understanding your values – those principles of living that truly matter to you – can explain why certain people or situations trigger frustration or anger. When someone behaves in a way that directly opposes a deeply held value of yours, it can feel confronting. At times, it may even feel like a personal attack.

This emotional discomfort is natural, but if you react with anger, resentment or defensiveness, there's a risk you'll end up acting in ways that further contradict your own values – deepening your discomfort and leaving you even more out of integrity. We'll explore specific strategies for managing these strong emotions in the next chapter, but for now, notice how much power there is in choosing not to be swept away by them.

Leading with Graceful Power means choosing to stay congruent, even when others are not. It's choosing to act in alignment with your own values, regardless of how others behave.

In her memoir *Becoming*,[1] Michelle Obama reflects on this tension. She describes a guiding principle she and Barack hold: "When they go low, we go high." Dignity, she believes, is a choice – often not the easiest one, but one that allows you to stay true to yourself.

Yes, some people act thoughtlessly or even maliciously. But more often, what feels like disrespect is simply someone living by different values. When two people are paired on a project – one who prioritizes risk-taking and the other who values security – sparks may fly. Yet if each of them can articulate their own values and hear the other person's values with respect, they can design how to make their partnership work, and even how the outcome may benefit from their two different perspectives.

This reframe can help you respond with curiosity rather than judgement. I often remind myself of this when someone fails to meet a commitment to me. Honouring a commitment is a core value for me. Instead of quickly labelling them flaky, I try to imagine what personal value they may have been prioritizing – perhaps care for a family member or excellence on another project. This helps to release the personal sting and allows me to respond more productively.

Values as guides, not rules

It's important to remember that your values are yours. They are not universal truths or moral rules. They represent the preferences and principles that help you navigate life meaningfully. When held too tightly, even a noble value can become a rigid standard that leads to judgement, shame or inner conflict.

Case study: From rigidity to responsibility

When I first met Robin, the Chief Strategy Officer of a multinational technology firm, we began with a conversation about his values. He was clear on one in particular: he valued calm, rational, emotion-free expression. It was essential, he said, to work with people who shared this approach. If someone expressed strong emotion, particularly anger, he found it deeply unsettling.

He explained that he himself avoided emotional expression at all costs. This made sense, as I had noticed how he would describe his delight or disappointment with the same measured tone and facial expression.

"So, you're remarkably even-keeled", I offered.

"Until I explode!" he replied.

As we talked more, this insight became a revelation.

It turned out Robin's father had an unpredictable temper. As a child, Robin had learned to stay quiet and suppress his feelings to avoid an outburst. As an adult, this survival strategy had evolved into a core value: *emotional control.* Behind it was a deep determination never to make anyone – particularly his own children – feel unsafe in his presence.

But it had become more than a preference. It had calcified into a rule.

If others broke that rule – if they got angry or raised their voices – Robin judged them harshly. And when he broke it himself, he judged himself even more. That occasional "explosion" he mentioned happened rarely, but when it did, it was dramatic – and left him feeling ashamed and conflicted.

This insight was freeing. Robin realized that emotional expression wasn't the enemy. He began to see emotion as a spectrum, not the binary choice of calm or enraged. He could honour his desire for emotional steadiness without denying his feelings entirely. Over time, he reframed his value from *emotional control* to *emotional responsibility – being aware of my impact on others.*

This new articulation allowed for greater authenticity and flexibility. Robin could still value composure, but he no longer saw emotional expression as weakness – in himself or others. In time, he became more open, more curious and more effective as both a leader and a parent.

As you reflect on your values, remember: they are precious, but they are not fixed. They are your guide, not your armour. Hold them lightly enough to evolve with you.

Your values can lead you to a life that feels aligned, fulfilling and whole. But if they harden into rules, they become rigid – limiting your growth, your relationships and your capacity for compassion.

Let them breathe as they guide you and grow with you.

VISUALIZING YOUR FUTURE SELF

Now that you have identified and begun working with your values to keep you on track, we'll look forward. The next exercise is a chance to imagine the leader you are becoming – the person who will carry these values into the future with wisdom, courage and compassion. If your values are your compass, your Future Self is the horizon: a steady point to move towards as you make daily choices.

I first encountered a Future Self visualization early in my coaching journey. I found it profoundly reassuring and inspiring in equal measure. It gave me a glimpse of what was possible, of where my life could go. It provided a clarity which was calming and a focus on the future that gave me a helpful perspective when dealing with day-to-day tribulations.

Since then, I've invited almost every client to visualize their Future Self. It offers a beautiful way to step out of the noise of daily life and explore who you are becoming, and the way of living you most aspire to. It adds dimension to the map we began in the Values exercise – this time painting a clearer picture of the destination you're journeying toward.

Guiding clients through this visualization has led to moments that are moving, enlightening and deeply personal. Although I won't be there to guide you in person, I'm so pleased to be able to share an audio recording with you, via the QR code in the Introduction.

Before you begin, here are a few tips to help you get the most from the process.

- The whole experience will take around 25–30 minutes. Set yourself up for success: choose a time when you won't be interrupted. Silence all notifications. Make yourself physically comfortable – lie on your bed, stretch out on the sofa or curl up in your favourite chair.
- Of the hundreds of clients I've taken through this visualization, experiences vary widely. Some see every detail vividly. Others are simply left with a sense, a feeling or a single phrase. Most people fall somewhere in between these two outcomes – even those who claim: "I'm terrible at this kind of thing!".
- To benefit fully, temporarily set aside that brilliantly rational, logical part of your mind and adopt a willingness to explore a more subconscious aspect of yourself. Relax and be curious about the experience.
- There's no right or wrong outcome. You'll receive whatever insight is most useful to you at this moment in your life.

- The first part of the exercise simply involves relaxing, and letting the words guide your thoughts. If your mind drifts, just notice and gently return your attention to my voice.
- After the visualization, you'll need 10–15 minutes to reflect and capture what came up, using the questions that follow. So have your notebook and pen nearby.

Ready? Don't read ahead to the reflection questions. Go straight to the audio recording and come back here afterwards.

Future Self reflections

How was your journey to the future?

Your experience of your Future Self is a resource – a way to lift out of the everyday and check that you're on track to becoming the person you truly want to be.

Use the following questions to reflect and note down the details, insights, impressions or messages that emerged. If the answer to a particular question wasn't revealed during the visualization, try imagining what the answer might be now. Stay with the feeling and energy of the visualization until you've captured everything important.

1. Where in the world did you find yourself?
2. What did your Future Self's home and the surrounding environment look and feel like?
    - What could you see, hear, smell?
    - What time of year was it? What was the weather like?
    - What do you sense was nearby, even if you didn't see it directly?
3. Describe the home – its size, style, character, position.

4. As your Future Self greeted you:
   - What were your first impressions?
   - How did they look, dress and greet you?
   - How did it feel to be with them in their home environment?
5. Describe the interior of the home – the colours, furnishings and atmosphere. What do these details tell you about the kind of person who lives here?
6. What did you notice about how your Future Self moved through their home, their posture, energy or attitude?
7. Where did you sit and talk? Were you offered something to drink?
8. What kind of person is your Future Self?
   - How would you describe them?
   - How do they relate to others?
   - How do they view the world?
9. What was your Future Self's response to these questions:
   - "What has been most meaningful and memorable for you in the past 20 years?"
   - "What do I need to know to ease my progress from where I am today to where you are?"
10. Did you ask any other questions? What answers did you receive?
11. What was the gift your Future Self gave you? What message or meaning does it hold for you?

When you've finished your notes, take a short break, then come back for the next part of the exercise.

Accelerating progress

Now that you've glimpsed your Future Self, would you like to fast-track your progress? Would you like to begin drawing their qualities into your present-day self?

If the answer is yes, let's turn that intention into a plan for change.

Step 1: Letting go

To become more like your Future Self, what three patterns of thought or behaviour do you need to leave behind?

1.

2.

3.

Step 2: Taking up

What three ways of thinking or acting can you take up today that would bring you closer to this vision?

1.

2.

3.

Step 3: Visualizing the shift

If you commit to these changes now, how might your life change? What would shift for you and perhaps for those around you?

Step 4: Getting honest

How do you feel about these changes? Excited? Hopeful? Fearful? Embarrassed?

What advice might your Future Self give you to help you begin?

Here's my advice: commit to making these changes imperfectly. Be willing to be a beginner. You won't get it right every time – but keep going. With repetition, your old habits will soften and new ones will take hold.

Step 5: Demonstrating commitment

1. Identify three ways you will now behave differently. Write down what you will stop doing and what you will do instead.
2. Within five days, acquire the gift from your visualization – or a symbolic equivalent. Choose something tangible that reminds you of this commitment.
3. Say out loud the three behaviours you're leaving behind and the three you're adopting. Share them with a trusted friend. If that feels too vulnerable, simply share with the bathroom mirror. The key is to hear yourself declare it – and mean it.

Now note your observations and commitments into your Code of Congruence.

A note on difficult visions

Very occasionally, a client sees a negative vision of the future – one that feels far from what they hoped. If that happened for you, don't worry.

Rather than seeing this as a failure, consider it a message. Could the vision be showing you what might happen if your current patterns continue unchecked? What might it be asking you to change?

Draw what learning you can. Sit with it. Wait a few days, and when you're ready, try the visualization again. With reflection, your subconscious may reveal a clearer, more aligned path forward.

CRAFTING YOUR LEADERSHIP SIGNATURE

Having connected with your Future Self, you've glimpsed the leader you are growing into. To deepen this insight, the next step is to look outward – exploring how the choices and behaviours of other leaders can inform your own. This exercise will help you refine your Leadership

Signature: the distinctive combination of qualities that will shape your presence, your impact, and the way others experience you as a leader.

Those who lead with Graceful Power observe the leadership of others with curiosity and discernment. They draw inspiration from what they admire and clarity from what they would never choose to emulate. They look for insight into how to improve their own presence and impact, while staying true to their values.

There is almost always something to learn from the leadership of others – if we're willing to look with an open mind. Even those we dislike or disagree with can offer lessons. You can probably think of a public figure whose judgement you consider flawed yet who demonstrates real effectiveness as a leader, or someone who seems kind-hearted and well-intentioned but struggles to lead with impact.

When you watch a film, read the news, attend a sports match or join a community meeting, take a step back from the outcome and focus on the people shaping events. Some will hold formal leadership roles – captain, manager, chair, director. Others will lead from within the group, influencing the atmosphere or culture through their contribution. Ask yourself:

- What is this leader doing or saying – or *not* doing and saying – that's influencing this situation?
- What could I learn from this?
- If I applied this behaviour to my own leadership, how would things change?

Our society loves heroes and villains. When things go wrong, the question "Who's to blame?" is often aimed at people in positions of responsibility. It's a question that tends to close conversations down, pushing people onto the defensive. And in doing so, we lose valuable learning.

That's not to say leaders shouldn't be held accountable. But in a culture of Graceful Power, we make space for leaders to be human. We learn from both their successes and their stumbles, and we become wiser leaders ourselves as a result.

Exercise: Crafting your Leadership Signature

This exercise will help you identify the leadership attributes you most admire. It offers a view of what you aspire to, and where your development could most usefully focus.

You'll need about 30 minutes, plus your notebook and pen.

Step 1: Choose your leaders

Identify three leaders you admire deeply. They can be people you know personally or public figures. They can be alive or dead, real or fictional, from any context – business, politics, arts, family, film. From your grandmother to Gandhi to Gandalf, no one is off the table. The only criterion is that you admire their leadership approach.

Step 2: Build your attribute list

For each of your three chosen leaders, write a long list of qualities you admire about their approach to leadership. Don't focus on *what* they've achieved, but *how* they achieved it. This is about your personal perception, not factual accuracy.

- Start with the first person and list everything you admire. The first few traits will come easily, then you'll need to dig a little deeper. When you think you're done, broaden your perspective and see if you can find two or three more traits.
- Repeat this process with your second and third leaders. Repetition is fine – some traits may appear across all three. Capture everything.

Step 3: Create your ideal leader

Now, imagine you have the power to create your ideal leader. Someone who consistently exhibits the *five* traits you admire most from your list.

- Review your full list.
- Highlight or circle the "no-brainers".

- Then challenge yourself to choose between the rest until you've selected the five traits or leadership qualities that most powerfully resonate with you.

Step 4: Write your Leadership Signature

At the top of a fresh page in your notebook, write the statement:

I am at my most inspiring and impactful as a leader when I...

Beneath this, list the five attributes you selected, rewriting them as full, active phrases. Adjust grammar as needed to create a confident, coherent statement that reflects your unique leadership identity. Don't soften the phrasing to make this a more comfortable list. Describe the traits in yourself just as you did when describing the leaders you had in mind. Even if this doesn't feel true of you – yet.

Example

I am at my most inspiring and impactful as a leader when I...

- have laser focus on the vision of my business
- do what is right, even when it's unpopular
- show resilience and remain calm in uncertainty
- connect with people at a deeply human level
- help others achieve more than they ever thought possible

Step 5: Reflect and activate

Read your full Leadership Signature out loud. Then read it again – this time like you *really* mean it.

- How does it feel to claim these qualities for yourself?
- Which ones feel natural and familiar?
- Which make you feel shy, anxious or stretched?

Ask yourself:

- What would change in my leadership approach if I consciously embodied these five traits?
- What would become easier?
- What would become harder?
- How might people respond differently to me?
- How would I feel at the end of each day?

Step 6: Ten-day practice

For the next ten days, observe the impact of carefully and consciously exhibiting these signature behaviours.

Days 1–5: Focus on one of your five traits each day. Lean-in with intention. Experiment. Notice what shifts in how you lead, how you feel and how others respond.

Days 6–10: Before each meeting, call or interaction: pause and choose the trait that will be most useful. Carry it into the moment with you. Afterwards, reflect:

- How well did I exhibit that trait?
- How did it shape my contribution and the outcome?
- What will I do differently next time?

After the ten days, return to your Leadership Signature and ask yourself:

- Which of these qualities am I living most comfortably and consistently?
- Which still need more focus and commitment?

Now you can add your Leadership Signature to your Code of Congruence.

Remember, this isn't about becoming someone else – it's about becoming more fully yourself in your leadership. Keep practicing and learning, even when things don't quite go to plan – this is often where the most useful learning lies.

CLARIFYING YOUR PURPOSE

So, you've explored your values, envisioned your Future Self and distilled the leadership attributes you most want to embody. Together, these give you clarity about who you are and how you want to lead. The next step is to connect this picture to something bigger than yourself: your sense of purpose.

A clear sense of purpose is a critical component of congruent leadership. It brings coherence, direction and resilience to a leader's actions – especially when the going gets tough. Leaders who act with purpose know what drives them and what they are working towards – personally and organizationally. This kind of clarity fuels Graceful Power: the capacity to lead with both strength and alignment. It is a sense of purpose that weaves a red thread through decisions, behaviour and impact.

What do we mean by purpose? Most of us start with a baseline motivation: we work to earn a living – to meet our needs and support those who depend on us. But if financial reward is our only driver, we'll likely do just enough to get by.

To show up fully in our work – with creativity, resilience and commitment – we need something more. We need to believe that our efforts contribute to something that matters.

Purpose is the answer to the question: In service of… what?

- I'm willing to hear difficult feedback and grow *in service of…*
- I push through long hours and uncertainty *in service of…*
- I stay patient with challenging people *in service of…*

When we work in the pursuit of something meaningful, we unlock a kind of discretionary energy that money alone can't buy.

Alignment with organizational purpose

Congruent leaders align their personal purpose with the function of their role and with the purpose of their team and organization. Within a team, this creates a shared sense of direction and a deeper level of commitment.

Take the example of a food manufacturer whose purpose is to eliminate single-use plastic within ten years. Each leader on the team is united by this shared goal, but driven by different personal motivations:

1. Leaving the planet better than they found it.
2. Tackling exciting innovation challenges.
3. Deepening their expertise.
4. Building their industry reputation.
5. Being part of a united, values-led team.
6. Providing long-term financial security for their family.

Their alignment doesn't come from having identical sources of motivation, but from connecting their own individual purpose to the shared one.

We'll explore organizational alignment further in the next chapter. For now, let's focus on defining your personal purpose.

Guidance for clarifying your purpose

Leaders describe their sense of purpose in many different ways. Some call it their north star, true north or guiding light. Others talk about their mission, vision or simply their "why". In this book, I use the word purpose because of its emotional resonance and its direct link to purposeful leadership. But there's no single right descriptor – choose the language that feels most meaningful to you.

You may have seen public purpose statements distilled into beautifully crafted single sentences. If you can write one, fantastic. But don't worry if you can't. Purpose is rarely something you nail in one sitting. It's layered, evolving and deeply personal. It doesn't have to be neatly packaged to be meaningful or useful to you.

The process of defining your purpose works best as an open, ongoing inquiry rather than a hunt for a single "right" answer. Draw insights from the Values, Future Self and Leadership Signature exercises you've completed, as well as from the exercise that follows. A mind-mapping technique can be especially helpful here, allowing you to spot unexpected links and patterns that a simple list might miss.

One thing to watch for: avoid chasing the purpose you think you *should* have. This is not about impressing others or gaining their approval. Your purpose is for *you*. It only needs to be authentic, meaningful and motivating to *you* – nobody else.

Finally, let your emotions be a guide. If the description of your purpose energizes you, feels rewarding to pursue, and stirs a mix of pride and a little trepidation, you're on the right track. Purpose doesn't have to be perfect from the start. You'll continue shaping and refining it over time, letting the detail become clearer as you learn more about yourself and the impact you want to have.

Exercises to clarify your purpose

Clarifying your purpose begins with recognizing the themes, motivations and desired outcomes that give your leadership meaning.

The following four exercises are designed to help you explore your unique sense of purpose from a range of different angles. Each offers a different lens to examine what you stand for, what drives you and what you hope your leadership will ultimately serve. Take your time working through each in turn. Making notes of the thoughts, ideas and insights that come to you. Later you will pull these notes together in a more coherent form. For now, approach these exercises with curiosity, giving yourself time to reflect deeply. You might find that two or three are particularly revealing, but give each a chance as even a small, insight can bring fresh clarity.

Exercise 1: The birthday tribute

Imagine yourself many years from now, at a milestone celebration late in your life – a big, joyful gathering held entirely in your honour. The room is full of people from across the decades and different chapters of your life: family, friends, colleagues, mentors, teammates and others whose paths you've touched along the way.

As part of the celebration, a younger person close to you – perhaps a grandchild, niece, nephew or family friend – has compiled a video tribute made up of short messages from the guests. One by one, they answer questions such as:

- How would you describe [your name]?
- How did [your name] shape or influence you?
- Which of their achievements had the most lasting impact?
- What do you believe has brought them the deepest satisfaction across their life?

As the video plays clear themes emerge – threads that run through the stories people tell about you and the difference you've made. Take a moment and allow yourself to dream about who appears in this video and what they say.

- What themes do you hope or expect would be revealed?
- What would you be most proud and deeply fulfilled to hear reflected back about your life, your leadership and the impact you've had?

Make notes on your reflections. These imagined voices from your Future Self's celebration can offer powerful clues about the legacy you want to create, and the purpose that drives you today.

Exercise 2: Understanding your motivation

This exercise draws on the work of James Sale, who, through extensive research into human motivation, has identified nine core motivators that drive people in their work. In his book, *Mapping Motivation*,[2] he describes how energized and fulfilled we feel when our work aligns with our dominant motivators.

Each of us has a unique blend of these motivators, but usually two or three dominate and drive the majority of our energy and decisions. Purpose often sits at the intersection of what you care deeply about and where you naturally feel motivated to act.

As you read through the descriptions below, notice which ones resonate most strongly, spark an emotional response or describe situations where you feel most alive and fulfilled.

- Attempt to rank each source of motivation in order of importance for you – from most important to least.
- Sometimes this is made easier by imagining you are forced to choose between jobs that only offer one source of motivation – what could you not live without?
- Give priority to identifying the most important two or three sources of motivation and the least important one or two – and considering what this reveals.

Motivation source	Ranking
Expertise Learning, competence and expertise motivate you. You're happiest when deepening your skills, solving complex problems, and being recognized for the knowledge and capability you bring to the table. **Relationships** You thrive when you feel connected, supported and part of a team. Relationships are your fuel and you're happiest when your workplace values collaboration, trust and mutual care. **Recognition** You're motivated by being seen, appreciated and respected for what you achieve. Public acknowledgement of your contributions matters – not for vanity's sake, but because it signals progress, influence and personal growth.	

Motivation source	Ranking
Responsibility Autonomy and authority energize you. You want to shape strategy, make decisions and have a direct influence over outcomes, thriving when you feel in charge. **Tangible reward** You're driven by financial success and a good standard of living. Progress is often measured in practical gains – salary, assets, lifestyle – and achieving these goals fuels your sense of accomplishment. **Impact** You're driven by making a difference and want to feel that your work truly matters. Satisfaction comes from contributing to something bigger than yourself – creating impact, helping others or leaving a positive legacy. **Innovation** You're energized by originality and the freedom to express new ideas. Whether designing, building or innovating, you thrive in environments where creativity is valued and there's space to explore possibilities. **Stability** You find motivation in security, consistency and predictability. Change can feel unsettling, so environments where roles, expectations and systems are clear allow you to perform at your best. **Independence** Autonomy is everything to you. You're motivated by the ability to set your own direction, make independent choices and create a lifestyle that reflects your personal values and priorities.	

Exercise 3: Exploring layers of purpose

Sometimes your purpose lives in layers. Try using this exploratory writing technique to reveal the different layers of your purpose.

- Grab your pen and notebook.
- For each of the layers listed below, read the prompts then set a five-minute timer and simply write without pausing, editing or judging.
- Let your thoughts flow onto the page exactly as they come – messy, incomplete and unfiltered.

Layer 1: Personal purpose

What matters most to you? What do you hope to gain or experience by giving your very best? This is the inner layer – your own source of meaning and energy.

Layer 2: Impact purpose

What difference do you want to make? How do you want to influence people, teams, organizations or systems for the better? Think about the ripple effects you'd love your actions to create.

Layer 3: Legacy purpose

What do you want to leave behind? When you move on from a role, project or even this stage of life, what do you hope endures because of your effort?

Once you've explored each layer, take a moment to capture the essence of what emerged in your writing by completing these sentences – without overthinking or polishing:

- *My personal purpose is...*
- *My impact purpose is...*
- *My legacy purpose is...*

Remember, this isn't about crafting perfect sentences. It's about capturing the threads of what drives you, what matters to you and where you want to make a difference. You'll revisit and refine these insights later in this chapter and beyond.

Exercise 4: Give your purpose a metaphor

A useful way to uncover the essence of your purpose is to imagine it as an archetype, creature or object – something that symbolizes the influence or impact you want to have on the world.

This is your chance to get creative. It doesn't need to sound clever, impressive or "worthy." It just needs to mean something to you. Often, the most surprising metaphors are the ones that open up the deepest insights.

Here are a few real-life examples from my clients:

- "I am a fairy godmother who helps others achieve what they couldn't alone."
- "I am a guiding light – steady and calm, always visible, leading the way."
- "I am the sledgehammer that smashes the barriers holding people back."
- "I am a feather duster that quietly tidies what others overlook."
- "I am a lioness that fiercely protects her pride."
- "I am the rock that provides a solid foundation others can build on."

Notice how each example captures both identity and impact – what they are and the difference they make.

Now, experiment with writing your own:

I am a [insert your metaphor] *that* [describe the difference you make].

Don't overthink it. Trust your instincts. The metaphor that comes to mind – even if it feels silly or strange – may reveal something powerful about who you are and the influence you want to have.

Pulling it together: Your working purpose statement

You now have plenty of raw material. It's time to shape it into a "good-enough" working statement of purpose. This can be a single phrase or a few sentences. Aim for meaningful over word-perfect.

Try this structure as a starter:

- *My purpose is to* .... [describe your action or behaviour]
- *Which will influence* .... [these people or system]
- *In this way* .... [the impact]
- *So that* .... [the outcome]

Quick tests for a "good enough" statement:

✓ Applies across your life – not just one role or period of time.
✓ Describes your influence – how you show up and what you bring.
✓ Names your impact – what changes because of you.
✓ Aligns with your values and who you're becoming.
✓ Feels like a stretch yet do-able – a little daunting, still realistic.
✓ Stirs emotion – pride, excitement, trepidation… maybe even a flicker of fear.

Examples

Here are a few examples of purpose statements to inspire your thinking. These aren't templates to copy, they are to help you shape a version that feels authentic to you. Each one is different in style and tone – some more metaphorical, some more practical – chose whatever approach feels most true to you.

> "My purpose is to inspire individuals to believe in themselves, helping them create lives of purpose and fulfilment. In doing so, I contribute to a world where more people live with confidence, resilience and joy."
>
> "My purpose is to use design and systems thinking to make education more empowering and accessible. Like a locksmith with the right keys, I open the doors to knowledge and possibility for those who've been locked out."
>
> "My purpose is to move through the world like a wolf – loyal, watchful and willing to walk first. My purpose is to protect and empower others so we rise together, stronger as a pack."
>
> "My purpose is to speak up for what matters and encourage others to do the same. Like a lantern-bearer lighting the path, I help others find the courage to step forward too."
>
> "My purpose is to build a business that stands the test of time. By delivering exceptional value and creating trust, I enable sustainable commercial success for everyone involved."
>
> "My purpose is to be a social innovator – part dreamer, part problem solver. By asking 'what if?' and daring to explore the answers, I help shape better ways to live, work and connect – turning imagination into everyday improvement."
>
> "My purpose is to build a life where family comes first and success is measured by connection, not accumulation. I want to model a way of living that's abundant, grounded and full of joy."

Don't lose your emotional connection with the statement by trying to craft a word-perfect version today. Making a start is what matters, you can keep refining as your understanding grows. Remember this statement is just for you, a reminder of what you feel energized and inspired to do.

Now you can add your purpose statement to your Code of Congruence.

We've covered a lot of ground in this chapter. Through a blend of introspection and practical application, I hope you've discovered more about yourself – and how you can influence and impact the people and systems around you.

You've clarified the core values you want to honour, envisioned the Future Self you aspire to become, defined the unique traits of your Leadership Signature style and deepened your connection to your sense of purpose – a source of both motivation and fulfilment.

If you've chosen to capture these insights in your Code of Congruence, you now have a tangible reminder of the essential ingredients that make you "you". A living framework to return to – grounding you when times feel turbulent, inspiring you when you feel lost, and guiding you when the way forward isn't clear.

Leading with Graceful Power calls for this ever-deepening self-awareness. It allows you to respond to challenges and opportunities with greater self-possession – choosing how you show up, rather than reacting on autopilot, so you create the best possible outcomes for yourself and those you lead.

In the next chapter, we'll take this a step further and explore one of leadership's greatest paradoxes: how to stay dependably true to yourself while remaining agile enough to adapt to the demands of your role. This is where we move from understanding yourself to developing authentic agility – the foundation for leading with influence, clarity and ease.

Chapter 6

Developing authentic agility

Equipped with the deeper self-knowledge gained in the previous chapter, you may already notice yourself leading with greater awareness and self-possession. You've identified the raw ingredients of your Graceful Power – the inner foundation that allows you to grow into the grounded confidence that comes from knowing who you are and what you stand for.

Now comes the real work: putting that knowledge into practice. The more self-possessed you become – meaning actively choosing *how* you show up in the world and the impact you have on others – the more congruent your leadership becomes. And the more congruent your leadership, the more naturally you inspire trust, respect and loyalty in those around you.

Yet this isn't simple. One of the greatest paradoxes of modern leadership is this: we must be consistently true to ourselves while continually adapting to serve the needs of our role, our organization and our teams. In other words, leaders are called to be both reliably consistent *and* reliably flexible.

Navigating this tension requires authentic agility: the ability to stay rooted in who you are while flexing your approach to meet the demands of each situation. In the moments when your personal values align beautifully with what's required, leadership can feel effortless – fluid, natural and energizing. But leadership also demands that we step into more complex spaces: asking for things we'd prefer not to, collaborating with people we don't easily relate to or making decisions that others may resist.

A gracefully powerful leader doesn't try to eliminate this tension – they learn to work *with* it. They adapt their behaviour without losing themselves. They bring intention to every interaction, adjusting both their practical and emotional contributions to create the best possible outcomes. They hold a strong sense of self without becoming trapped by a rigid definition of what that means.

Take Milly, for example. Honesty is one of her primary values – she believes it truly is the best policy. But through experience, she's learned that honesty takes many forms. It can be blunt and factual, or gentle and thoughtful. It can build someone up or tear them down. Acting with authentic agility, Milly stays true to her value of honesty in ways that serve both the individual and the broader purpose. She doesn't honour her value rigidly, but intentionally, communicating with care and respect in every situation.

In the pages ahead, we'll explore four specific practices that strengthen and sustain this kind of congruent, self-possessed leadership:

- Emotional mastery
- Leading with intention
- Continuous learning and improvement
- Finding cultural congruence

These practices will help you balance the two sides of the paradox: staying anchored in your identity while developing the agility to adapt and thrive in the complex realities of modern leadership.

EMOTIONAL MASTERY

Congruent behaviour calls for adept emotional management. Plans will fail. People will disappoint you. Sometimes, despite your best efforts, you'll fall short. Leaders with Graceful Power care deeply when things go wrong, but they work hard to avoid being hijacked by their emotional response. That doesn't mean they don't feel things intensely – quite the opposite. Leading gracefully starts with granting yourself full permission to feel.

Emotional mastery isn't about suppressing your feelings; it's about noticing them clearly, understanding where they come from and choosing your response with intention. It's equally important when things go right. Success can throw us off-balance too, particularly when we're celebrating while others around us may be wrestling with frustration or failure. Graceful leaders regulate both their disappointment *and* their triumph, responding with empathy and awareness to the emotional energy in the room.

Why emotions matter in leadership

Over the years, I've worked with many talented, committed leaders who arrived at coaching feeling overwhelmed – caught on the emotional rollercoaster of daily life. Rushing from one meeting to the next, they carried the emotional hangover of previous interactions with them. Without time to reflect or process, they became increasingly reactive and volatile.

At the other extreme, I've met leaders who recount ongoing crises with a tight smile and strained laugh – outwardly displaying calm while describing deeply stressful situations. When asked how these events made them feel, they might offer only a flat "not good" or, at a stretch, "bad."

Both patterns – volatility and suppression – create distance and mistrust. There's something unsettling about someone describing a major challenge while smiling, just as it's destabilizing when a colleague's unpredictable moods dictate the tone of a meeting.

Recognizing and naming what you feel

How can you influence the emotions of others if you're overwhelmed by – or disconnected from – your own? Whether I'm working with someone emotionally volatile, emotionally muted or simply seeking greater congruence, the starting point is the same: learning to accurately identify and name what you're feeling.

As the saying goes: "If you can't name it, you can't tame it."

Specificity matters. Labels like "pretty good" or "a bit cross" don't tell you much about what's actually happening. What we're after is emotional granularity:

- "I feel pretty good" becomes "I feel proud/productive/energized/confident."
- "I'm a bit cross" becomes "I feel irritated/frustrated/resentful/trapped."

Studies by neuroscientist Dr Lisa Feldman Barrett[1] show that precise emotional labelling strengthens self-regulation, resilience and your ability to influence others' emotional engagement. The more accurately you understand what you're feeling – and why – the more power you have to choose your response and navigate similar emotions effectively in the future.

Some people do this naturally. Others need to build the skill deliberately. Either way, we can all improve.

Practising emotional awareness

If this feels challenging, begin by tuning into broad categories of emotion rather than trying to pinpoint exact labels straight away. In *Permission to Feel*,[2] Professor Marc Brackett introduces the Mood Meter, a simple yet powerful tool that groups emotions by two dimensions: their energy level (high or low) and how pleasant or unpleasant they feel. It's an accessible starting point – a stepping stone towards naming what you're experiencing more precisely.

Take a moment to notice the physical sensations present in your body right now – the subtle clues to your current emotional state:

- Are you feeling something pleasant and enjoyable that you'd like to savour, or an unpleasant, uncomfortable sensation you'd prefer to ease or avoid?
- Does the emotion feel mild and low in energy, or intense and highly charged?

Practise this over the coming weeks. A few times a day, pause and check in with yourself. Notice whether you feel comfortable or uncomfortable, and how strong or gentle those feelings are.

This simple act of noticing – slowing down long enough to ask, “How am I feeling right now?” – can have a surprisingly powerful effect on your leadership. It deepens your self-awareness, influences how you interact with others, and helps shape the emotional energy around you.

Then get specific: Grow your emotional vocabulary

As you build this habit, take the next step: move from simply identifying how your mood feels in your body to naming the exact emotion you’re experiencing.

For example:

- If you’re feeling an *unpleasant*, *high-energy emotion*, is it anxiety, stress, overwhelm, panic, frustration or something else?
- If you’re experiencing a *pleasant*, *low-energy emotion*, would you describe it as content, peaceful, relaxed, mellow or maybe relief?

For many of us, this level of precision feels unfamiliar. We simply don’t have the vocabulary to describe the nuances of what we’re experiencing – and without the right words, our ability to regulate emotions is limited.

One brilliant tool to help develop this skill is the *How We Feel*[3] app, based on Marc Brackett’s Mood Meter model. You check in, select your mood category and then choose from a menu of emotions, each with a clear definition. Personally, I thought I was already pretty good at recognizing how I felt – but using the app sharpened my awareness dramatically. Choosing between several closely related emotions in the same category forces you to pause, reflect and pinpoint your exact experience. That clarity helps you trace the emotion back to its trigger – the event, thought or interaction that set it off.

This is where the real power lies. When you stop and name exactly what you're feeling and why, you create a moment of self-awareness – a small pause that opens the gateway to better regulation, more intentional action and greater congruence in how you show up.

Build your practice further by articulating your emotion and the event that triggered it. For example:

- "I feel proud because I redirected our strategic focus without demotivating the team."
- "I feel frustrated and disappointed because Henry missed the deadline again."
- "I feel inadequate because everyone else in the room has more experience than me."

One of my clients, who struggled to recognize his feelings, decided to practise this skill with his young son. Each evening, they shared one pleasant and one unpleasant moment from their day and helped each other name the associated emotion. It became a bonding ritual, expanding both their emotional vocabularies and deepening their connection.

From awareness to influence

Assuming someone has the skills for the task, it's often how they *feel* about doing it that determines the quality of their work.

Imagine I'm running a conference, and the caterer has let me down at the last minute. I ask you to step in and organize lunch for 50 delegates. If I let my stress and frustration show and ask abruptly, you might feel resentful and disengaged. You'll do the job – but without care or pride.

But if I pause, acknowledge my upset and ask for your help in a way that makes you feel trusted and valued, the outcome will likely be far better.

The single greatest influence on the culture of a team is the behaviour of its leader – which includes the emotional tone they set. A CEO preparing for a board presentation who feels defensive after receiving criticism may unconsciously transmit that mood to their team. But if they can pause, acknowledge the feeling and reframe it – choosing to project calm confidence instead – their team is far more likely to prepare and perform with focus and ease.

Parable of the two arrows

When my sons were young, they were non-stop action, which meant frequent falls and grazed knees. What always struck me was how quickly they recovered. There'd be tears, hugs and plasters – and then they were off again, the incident forgotten. The magnitude of some of these scrapes, skidding across tarmac on their knees, would have left me rattled for hours. As an adult, I'd worry about healing, feel embarrassed about the undignified scene and run through endless "what ifs". Their resilience reminded me of a Buddhist parable.

Buddha asked his followers to imagine someone walking through a forest when an arrow pierces their chest. "What would that be like?" he asked. Everyone agreed it would be terrible.

Then he invited them to imagine the same person, sitting on the ground clutching the wound, when a second arrow strikes the same spot. "And what would that be like?" he asked. The followers cried, "Even worse!".

The first arrow represents the unavoidable pain of life's setbacks, crises and disappointments. The second arrow represents our own emotional response to the first arrow – the suffering we create ourselves: the rumination, blame, replaying of "what ifs", and spirals of self-criticism.

As leaders, we can't always avoid the first arrow. But we *can* choose whether we fire the second into ourselves creating further pain – this time self-inflicted.

Regulating your response

Recognizing what you feel is the starting point. But emotional mastery comes from what you do next: how you regulate and express those emotions in ways that serve your purpose and the people around you.

Following, are six techniques. Not all will suit everyone or every situation. Experiment until you find the ones that work for you.

Understanding fear to regulate emotion

Many of the emotions we find unpleasant or uncomfortable stem from *fear* – the fear of failure, rejection, loss or of having our vulnerability exposed. Becoming aware of this connection can be powerful. When we identify that fear is driving the intensity of what we feel, it becomes easier to name, work with and regulate those emotions.

We'll explore the human fear response in much greater depth in Chapter 8, including how your brain and body react when you sense threat and how you can work with, rather than against, those instincts.

Soothing your nervous system

Our "always-on" culture overstimulates body and mind. Building "buffer zones" into your routine helps you reset: walking in nature practicing mindfulness meditation or yoga; pursuing creative hobbies or simply stepping away from your desk to breathe deeply for two minutes. Purposeful distractions with tangible outcomes – cooking, gardening, writing, even reorganizing a messy drawer – can be surprisingly effective at restoring balance.

Stepping outside yourself

When someone's behaviour provokes strong feelings, it's easy to get hooked into your own story. Pause and ask: "What if this isn't about me?". Imagine yourself as a minor character in their narrative rather than the protagonist of your own. Curiosity about what might be going on for them often softens your reaction and creates space for better connection.

Decoding your body's signals

Dr Barrett's research suggests that emotions begin as the brain's "best guess" response to a situation based on past experience – and they tend to show up first in the body. Practice tuning into your body to notice changes in breathing, muscle tension and energy levels. Pretend you're describing these physical symptoms to a doctor: "My shoulders are tight, my jaw's clenched, my stomach's fluttery." These cues provide valuable data for regulation before emotions spiral.

Reframing your experience

Naming emotions with more precision can also change them. While writing this chapter, I was looking forward to a Friday afternoon with my now teenage sons, when their school closed after lunch. That morning, they messaged to say they'd made plans to spend the afternoon with friends instead of coming home. My disappointment triggered a cascade of dramatic thoughts: "They don't need me anymore! My life is empty!".

I opened the *How We Feel* app and labelled my emotion: "**Disappointed** – sad because my expectations weren't met". Then I explored other perspectives:

- **Respected:** they'd communicated clearly and trusted me to respond positively.
- **Proud:** I'm raising independent, sociable young men.
- **Wishful:** longing for time with them is natural.

My sense of disappointment softened. I sent them off warmly and enjoyed a riverside walk with my husband instead.

Resetting your energy

Sometimes, regulating emotion isn't about calming down – it's about reclaiming focus and vitality. Elite athletes do this constantly: transforming nerves into drive using music, rituals and movement. The New Zealand All Blacks perform the Haka, a traditional Māori war dance, before each rugby match. It unifies the team, channels adrenaline and transforms raw emotional energy into strength and purpose.

Your "reset" can be gentler: a playlist that lifts you, a breathing technique that steadies you, a mantra that centres you, or a brief meditation to refocus your mind. These micro-resets are tools to consciously shape the emotional state you bring to the next moment.

Putting emotional mastery into practice

Developing emotional mastery is an ongoing practice – one built through awareness, reflection and experiment. Each time you pause, name what you feel, and choose your response intentionally, you strengthen your Graceful Power. You also set the emotional tone for those around you, creating the psychological safety people need to do their best work.

Mastering your emotions doesn't make you less human. It makes you more present, more grounded and more influential. It allows you to lead with intention, not impulse.

It lays the foundation for what comes next. Once you can manage your own emotions, you unlock the capacity to shape the behaviours, beliefs and performance of others. In the next section, we'll explore how to use your emotional steadiness to create purposeful and intentional impact – shaping outcomes and cultures with clarity, compassion and confidence.

LEADING WITH INTENTION

Having explored emotional mastery – understanding, naming and regulating your own emotional state – the natural next step is to turn outward. Graceful Power isn't only about knowing yourself; it's about using that awareness intentionally to shape your impact on others and on the systems around you.

Being clear on your purpose and values as a leader is vital – but clarity alone isn't enough. It only becomes powerful when it's expressed through your impact: the way you influence the people and systems around you. Gracefully powerful leaders don't just *mean well*; they *act on purpose*, consciously shaping their influence with intention.

This intentionality is one of the most subtle yet effective traits of graceful leadership: the clear-sighted determination to ensure that your words, actions and energy are aligned with the outcome you hope to achieve.

Owning your impact

We often hear children say, "I didn't do it on purpose, it was an accident," when they've caused harm – broken something, hurt someone, said the wrong thing. The implication is that if the impact was unintentional, they shouldn't be held fully responsible.

Congruent leaders take the opposite approach. With the emotional maturity to own their impact, they pause to consider what's needed from an interaction – and what they must bring to it to make that outcome more likely. They take responsibility for the signals they send, the energy they bring and the influence they create.

Begin with the emotional end in mind

The secret to purposeful, intentional impact is to begin with the *emotional* end in mind. Before any important interaction – whether it's a team meeting, one-to-one conversation or a presentation – pause to reflect on four deceptively simple questions:

1. What do I want the other person or people to *do* as a result of this interaction?
2. How do I want them to *feel* as they do it – so they give it their best?

3. How do *I* need to *feel* to influence their emotional state effectively?
   (Hint: it's often the same feeling you want to generate in them.)
4. What do I need to *do* to get myself into that state, so I can show up fully and have the desired impact?

Notice that question two is about how they'll *feel*, not what they'll think. That distinction is critical. This isn't about manipulating others – it's about *managing yourself*. By consciously preparing your energy, presence and intent, you create the conditions that make the outcome you seek far more likely.

A useful technique is to picture the moment after the interaction ends. Imagine the other person pushing back their chair or clicking "Leave Meeting". How do you want them to *feel* in that moment? Energized? Supported? Focussed? Empowered? Challenged?

Too often, meetings begin before we've decided what we actually want from them. By the time we've found our focus, the moment has already passed, and our emotional presence has shaped the space – for better or worse. Gracefully powerful leaders don't leave that to chance. They prepare intentionally, ensuring their impact reflects their purpose.

The art of influence

This level of intentionality demands emotional ownership. Leaders with authentic agility take responsibility for how they show up, consciously shaping the emotional climate of an interaction to move people in the most useful direction – with greater ease, trust and speed.

Maya Angelou said it best:

> "I've learned that people will forget what you said,
> people will forget what you did,
> but people will never forget how you made them feel."

Intentionality isn't just about clarity of *message* – it's about clarity of *energy*. Congruent leaders choose the state they bring into the room.

They align how they feel with what they want others to feel. That's the real art of influence.

Whatever you bring to an interaction – whether intensely present or half-distracted, positively energizing or quietly undermining – will shape the outcome. So, shape it on purpose.

Your presence shapes culture

The single greatest influence on the culture of a team or organization is the behaviour of its leaders. Over time, every team develops a shorthand: "This is how we do things around here."

But in truth, it often translates to something more specific: "This is how our leaders do things around here."

When your daily presence is intentional, it sends signals. Over time, those signals become habits. And habits shape culture.

Case study: Clare Hornby – leading with relentless congruence

Clare Hornby launched Me+Em in 2009 with a clear mission: to help women feel confident in high-quality, flattering, fashionable clothes that last. From a small online collection, Clare has built one of the UK's fastest-growing fashion brands, with loyal customers worldwide and a growing network of physical stores in both the UK and the US.

At the heart of Clare's success is her obsessive attention to understanding her customers. When you meet her, it's clear she's one of life's quiet observers – noticing how women move through their days, juggle roles, and how clothes either help or hinder them. That vigilance drives both product innovation and customer loyalty.

As a leader, Clare demonstrates that same discipline with her team. She makes the centrality of the customer visible and explicit, communicating it in every decision and expecting the same focus from her team.

In the early days, staff absorbed the customer-focused culture organically by watching her in action. As the business scaled, Clare introduced systems to ensure the message cascaded. At monthly town hall meetings, she talks all employees through her one-page strategy, revisits progress against objectives and reconnects everyone to the brand's core customer profiles. Every team member understands the mission, and how their role supports it.

Clare also prioritizes her own time toward the areas of greatest customer impact. When opening stores in the US, she spent weeks immersed in her target neighbourhoods, walking the streets, observing lifestyles, eating where her future customers ate – absorbing their environment to ensure the launch would feel natural and effortless.

When new directors join, Clare personally coaches them in the nuances of the Me+Em ethos. She knows culture is too important to delegate, and too subtle to trust to onboarding documents alone.

The result? A team she trusts and that trusts her. A brand trusted by customers. And a leadership presence that's entirely congruent: who she is, what she says, how she behaves and what she expects are perfectly aligned.

One small but telling detail: no matter the fabric or factory, Me+Em's navy blue is *always* the same shade. Customers know any navy item they buy will match every other one in their wardrobe. That's brand congruence – rooted in leadership congruence. The details matter, and Clare ensures they're never left to chance.

Case study: Leadership by accident

Some years ago, I was approached by Martijn, one of the founders of a Dutch product design agency. The agency had grown quickly, earning a reputation for being agile, innovative and refreshingly different. Its culture attracted bright, creative disruptors hungry to do bold work for bold clients.

But success brought frustration. Despite strong values and a clear vision, the founders were struggling with their team's behaviour: missed meetings, chronic lateness, distracted attention and a lack of follow-through. The more the founders pointed out these issues, the less anything seemed to change.

I agreed to meet all four partners off-site, in a stylish Amsterdam members' club. The setting was elegant and quiet – perfect for a deep, reflective conversation. But as 11 am came and went, only one founder had arrived, and promptly stepped out again to take a call. The others trickled in over the next 20 minutes, pausing to finish messages or take calls in the anteroom. By 11:30 am, we still hadn't had all four of them in the room at once. Finally, one declared an emergency and left altogether.

As I sat observing, it became clear: I wasn't about to have a conversation about how their employees were misbehaving. I was about to have a conversation *about them*, and how their leadership behaviours were setting the tone for everything else. Their actions were speaking far louder than their words.

To their credit, the founders were open to this mirror being held up. We worked together to define the culture they wanted as they scaled – one that still honoured creativity and agility but introduced just enough structure to prevent chaos. It was never going to be corporate or rigid, but they began showing up with more presence, more consistency and more accountability.

They learned that whenever frustration bubbled up about a team behaviour, the first question to ask was: "How are we modelling this?".

They didn't become perfect, but they became more conscious. More congruent. More impactful. And the agency went from strength to strength – still unique, still agile, but now a little more *on purpose*.

Leading on purpose is a practice

Gracefully powerful leaders don't leave their impact to chance. They take responsibility not just for what they do, but for how they show up – aligning their energy, intentions and actions with the outcomes they want to create.

This isn't a one-time decision; it's a continual practice. Leading on purpose requires curiosity, reflection and a willingness to grow.

The next step? Learning how to stay in that process – evolving your leadership with the same intention you bring to every interaction.

Next, we'll explore Continuous Learning and Improvement: how to embed learning, build resilience and keep strengthening your Graceful Power over time.

CONTINUOUS LEARNING AND IMPROVEMENT

Leading on purpose means being intentional about your words, your energy and the impact you have on others. However, even the most conscious preparation can't guarantee the outcome you envisioned. That's why the next step in developing your Graceful Power is building the habit of learning from your experiences – reflecting on what happened, what worked and what you might do differently next time.

It's just as important to reflect and learn from your interactions as it is to prepare for them. There are lessons to be found in every successful conversation, every underwhelming meeting and every disastrous presentation – if you create the space to notice them.

The power of reflection

Human nature has a tendency to dwell on what went wrong. Many of us find endless time to beat ourselves up over perceived shortcomings. But far fewer of us pause to ask: "What did I do well that I must remember to do again next time?". And yet, building on your strengths is not only more effective but also far easier than trying to eliminate every weakness.

No matter how intentionally you lead, you won't always achieve the exact outcome you imagined. You might have prepared well, honoured your values and managed your emotions – and still found the conversation went sideways. That might be down to you, the other person, the dynamics between you or external factors entirely outside anyone's control. Most often, it's a mix of all of these.

Taking responsibility for your own contribution – and its impact – is what empowers you to learn and adapt. Authentic agility isn't something you're born with; it's a skill you develop through consistent reflection and iteration. The more consciously you practise, the more naturally it becomes part of your leadership approach.

Sometimes, it's the smallest shifts that make the biggest difference. Arriving at a meeting with a calm presence and a warm smile sets a very different tone to walking in late, frowning and preoccupied. Be alert to these moments – in yourself and in others – and make a note of them. What you notice is what you can learn from.

Case study: The energy you bring shapes the room

My client, Toby, discovered he was unintentionally injecting urgency and tension into his weekly team meetings. Driven by his own pressure to move quickly and deliver results, he noticed the team was rushing decisions rather than thoughtfully exploring the best options together.

To shift this dynamic, he experimented with a simple change. Before the weekly meeting, he blocked out 15 minutes to decompress – stepping away from his screen, making a hot drink and taking a few deep breaths. He deliberately brought himself into a calmer, more grounded state.

When the meeting began, he opened differently too – asking about everyone's weekend and what their week ahead looked like.

He'd hoped for a subtle improvement, but the effect was dramatic. The team visibly relaxed. People breathed. They smiled. The tone shifted from hurried to reflective, and the conversation became noticeably more collaborative and thoughtful.

A small change in his state had unlocked a big change in theirs.

The energy you bring into a room will change the energy of that room. Reflection allows you to notice the impact you're having – intentionally or not – and adjust how you show up next time. That's where growth happens.

The learning cycle

To embed this habit of learning, use this simple four-step reflection cycle adapted from Kolb's Experiential learning cycle.[4] It can take as little as two minutes after a quick conversation, or longer after a higher-stakes interaction, like a major presentation or sensitive one-to-one.

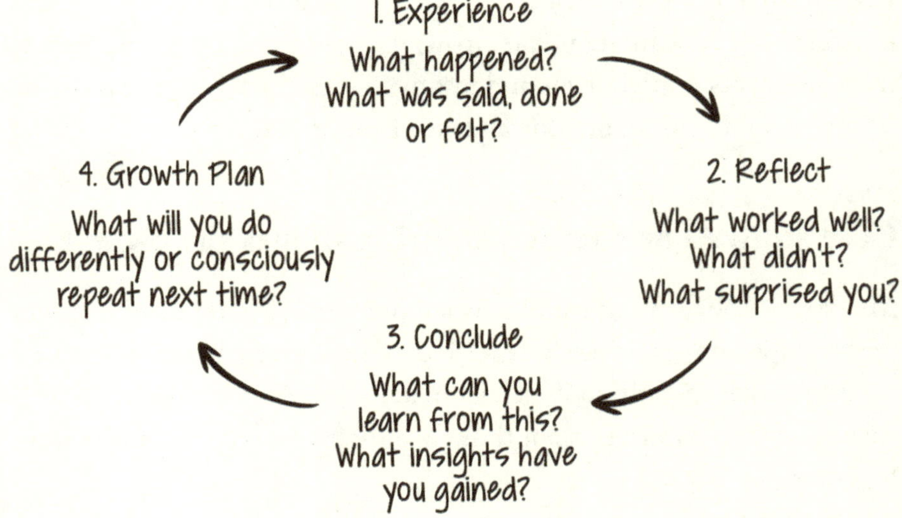

To get the most from this cycle of reflection and iteration

- **Capture insights quickly:** Scribble a few notes straight after the interaction – it helps embed the learning while it's fresh.
- **Apply it to what worked, not just what didn't:** Be as intentional about repeating success as you are about avoiding mistakes.
- **Don't aim for perfection; aim for evolution:** This is about staying in motion – learning, adapting and experimenting as you go.
- **Support yourself:** Use small reminders to reinforce change: a calendar note, a sticky note on your desk or a trusted colleague giving you a nudge.

You won't get it right every time – and that's not the goal. Progress is what counts.

Gathering feedback

Your personal reflections will take you a long way – but you'll go further, faster when you pair them with feedback from others.

We all have blind spots. When your intent is to inspire, energize or galvanize your team, it's vital to know whether your impact matched your intention. You might believe you've communicated with warmth and clarity – but your team may have experienced it very differently.

That's why feedback is essential for continuous learning. We'll explore the art of giving and receiving feedback in more detail in Chapter 11, but for now, keep it simple. For example:

> "I'm keen to make our team meetings and one-to-ones as effective as possible. What's working well for you right now? What am I doing that's helpful – so I know to keep doing it? And if I could adjust one thing to be even more effective, what would you suggest?"

And then – and this is the bit that matters most – respond in a way that encourages future honesty. Whether the feedback is easy or uncomfortable to hear, the most graceful response is often the simplest: "That's helpful to know. Thank you."

Continuous improvement in practice

Leading with Graceful Power means committing to growth. When you reflect on your experiences, learn from what you discover, and adjust your approach, you become more intentional, more agile and more impactful over time.

This mindset of continuous learning creates a ripple effect. Your openness invites others to grow alongside you. Your willingness to adapt builds trust. Your commitment to self-awareness and refinement sets the emotional tone for the team and, eventually, the culture.

This isn't about proving you're flawless, it's about showing up as a leader who learns.

FINDING CULTURAL CONGRUENCE

When your personal values, aspirations and sense of purpose align with those of your organization, you unlock a powerful source of energy and resilience. Being fully yourself becomes more effortless when the culture around you values what you stand for – surrounding you with like-minded people and shared purpose. This is cultural congruence.

But alignment doesn't need to be complete – expecting this would be unrealistic and, ultimately, frustrating. What matters is having enough shared ground to feel welcome as your true self. Cultural congruence doesn't happen by accident, and it isn't the sole responsibility of your organization. Both the individual and the organization play a role in creating and maintaining it.

Organizations have a duty to act congruently – with employees, customers and stakeholders – and to live up to the values they promote. At the same time, employees – especially leaders – have a responsibility to act with integrity, doing their best to align with organizational values while staying true to themselves. On the difficult days, it's this deeper alignment that sustains motivation and keeps your leadership grounded.

How do you know whether you're truly aligned – or whether you're slowly drifting away from it? A regular self-check can help you stay on course and avoid sliding into quiet frustration or resentment.

The Alignment Audit: Six self-check questions

Use the prompts below to reflect on your fit, influence and intentionality within your current environment:

1. **Revisit your Code of Congruence:** What are you motivated to achieve? Which values matter most to you? Without self-awareness, it's hard to recognize true alignment – or spot when it's missing.
2. **Compare the organization's stated purpose with its actual priorities:** Look beyond the mission statement. How does the organization behave day to day? Are its declared values lived out in real decisions and actions?

3. **Identify shared ground:** Where do your motivations and the organization's goals overlap? Seek alignment in purpose and principles.
4. **Acknowledge gaps or tensions:** Perfect alignment is rare, even in a company you've founded. Ask yourself:
   - How can I influence the gaps?
   - How can I stay authentic without compromising what matters most?
5. **Consider the impact you want to have from within:** How could your personal purpose become a lever for positive change? Many leaders find deep satisfaction in shaping culture from the inside – even in imperfect environments. By leading with purposeful intention, how could you shape the culture around you?
6. **Check for long-term fit:** Can you flourish here while staying true to how you work best?
   - If not, what conversations could realign things?
   - Could this role be a valuable stepping stone?
   - What would make it a worthwhile step for both you and the organization?

Cultural congruence doesn't require total alignment, but it does require enough shared ground to ensure your integrity remains intact. The goal isn't to force-fit yourself into an environment that erodes you – it's to find (or shape) the space where your purpose can thrive and make a meaningful difference.

When culture shifts

Of course, organizations evolve. A change in leadership, strategy or market can alter a culture – sometimes subtly, sometimes dramatically. Local and regional differences can influence how values are expressed day to day. Sometimes, it's you who changes. A new life stage, personal growth or shifting priorities may leave what once felt aligned suddenly feeling off-course.

In other instances, misalignment appears quickly. You might accept a role that seemed like the perfect fit – only to discover the reality is very different from the glossy picture you were sold. Even with the best preparation, leaders sometimes find themselves in environments where their values no longer feel welcome.

Surviving an incongruent culture

Years ago, I accepted a leadership role in a growing business with high hopes. I believed my vision for the team and my way of working were fully aligned with the values and direction of the business. But between accepting the role and joining the company, there was a change of leadership, and with it, a significant cultural shift. Within months, the person who had hired me left, recognizing this was no longer a place he could flourish.

It took me much longer to reach the same conclusion. What I witnessed daily felt incomprehensible: values that had previously defined the organization were now being quietly discarded. I was working harder than ever before, yet felt I was moving backwards.

I often describe that period as feeling like a fish swimming desperately against the current, confused that no one else seemed to be swimming with me.

Sadly, I'm not alone in this. Many of my clients have shared similar stories: joining organizations with high hopes, only to find themselves on the outside, watching behaviours unfold that feel fundamentally wrong. Sometimes, despite their best efforts to influence change, they are faced with a painful decision: adapt to fit a culture that jars with their values, or move on to find a better fit.

Case study: Cultural reframe

Arun faced a similar situation when he joined a long-established multinational as CFO. He came from a high-energy agile environment where the finance team worked as collaborative partners across the business. His new CEO assured Arun this was exactly the culture they wanted to build.

But shortly after joining, Arun discovered the reality was different. The organization was highly siloed and hierarchical. The finance team was expected to "stay in its lane" and was met with resistance when trying to collaborate. Despite initial assurances, the CEO and board showed little appetite for change.

Frustrated and exhausted, Arun came to coaching feeling demoralized. He didn't want this role to be a failure, nor did he want to feel like he'd wasted this chapter of his career. With at least 12 months left in the role, he wanted to make the most of it – but not at the expense of his wellbeing.

Together, we worked through the Alignment Audit. Step by step, Arun rescaled the meaning of this role from "career-defining" to "stepping stone". He shifted his goal from "revolutionary CFO" to "influential contributor". That simple reframing relieved the pressure and gave him clarity.

We identified three high-impact areas where he could make a meaningful difference and focused his energy on securing the board's backing. But perhaps the biggest shift came from his mindset. Instead of judging his colleagues, Arun began seeing himself as a respectful traveller in a foreign land. As a keen traveller, he'd always approached new cultures with curiosity and respect – and now, he brought that same mindset to work.

While he didn't always agree with the organization's customs, he sought to understand them – and gently offered alternative perspectives grounded in his experience. The shift transformed his relationships. Colleagues became less defensive and more receptive. His confidence returned.

Arun set a quiet, powerful intention:

> "I will be elegantly influential in my leadership here. When I leave, I want to have earned the respect of my colleagues, feel proud of my contribution and be grateful for the growth I've gained."

The practice of staying aligned

When leaders manage themselves with awareness and integrity – even in imperfect environments – every step becomes purposeful, and every setback becomes a chance to realign.

Cultural congruence isn't about a flawless match between you and your environment. It's about making conscious choices, staying awake to who you are and doing your best to lead in alignment with your values. Noticing when you're drifting, recalibrating and continuing to lead with clarity and purpose. Every role, every meeting and every conversation can move you forward – if you approach it intentionally.

This chapter marks the final step in our exploration of congruence – one of the three interwoven qualities of Graceful Power. Across these three chapters, you've deepened your understanding of yourself, clarified your values and purpose, developed emotional mastery, explored intentional impact and learned how to navigate cultural alignment.

Leading with congruence means living and leading from the inside out. It's about being grounded in who you are, consistent in what you stand for and intentional in the influence you create. When your inner compass is steady, your leadership presence becomes a source of trust, clarity and inspiration for those around you.

Congruence is never "done". It's a dynamic practice – a continual process of noticing, reflecting and realigning as both you and the world around you evolve.

In the next part of this book, we'll build on this as we turn to courage – exploring how to step beyond your comfort zone, confront fear and take the bold actions that define gracefully powerful leadership.

PART III

COURAGE

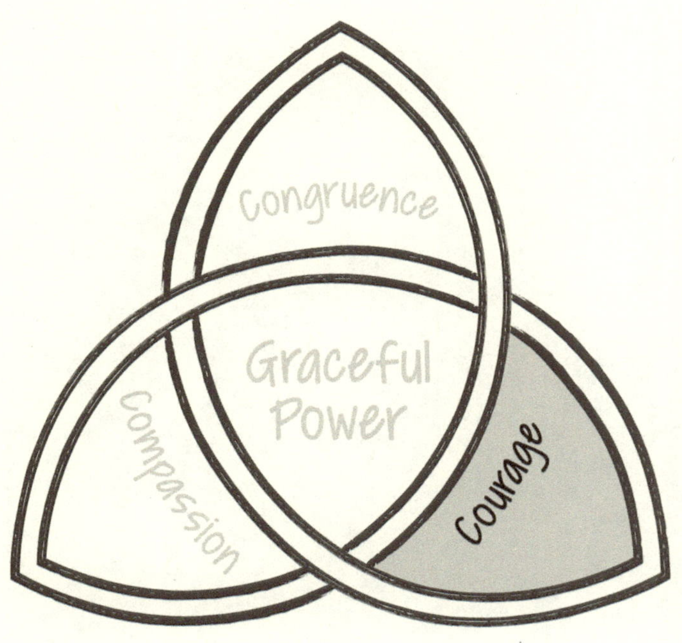

In this part of the book, we'll explore how courage supports you in balancing the challenges and tensions you face as a modern leader, and how it enables you to step into your Graceful Power:

- Chapter 7 – *The role of courage in Graceful Power.* We'll explore what courageous leadership looks like today and why it's so critical in navigating the competing demands and paradoxes of modern leadership.
- Chapter 8 – *Understanding fear.* Here, we'll look at why fear is a natural part of leadership and how it shapes your thoughts, feelings and behaviours more than you might realize. You'll learn to recognize its influence and see its role more clearly.
- Chapter 9 – *Managing fear and unlocking courage.* Finally, you'll learn practical strategies to manage fear skilfully, along with simple but powerful techniques to help you access your inner steadiness and choose courageous action when it matters most.

By the end of this section, you'll have a deeper understanding of what drives your courage, what holds it back and how to act with intention even when the outcome is uncertain. Courage helps you move forward with clarity and conviction, and when combined with congruence and compassion, it unlocks the full potential of your Graceful Power.

Chapter 7

The role of courage in Graceful Power

Leadership demands courage. Not the Hollywood kind – no swords, no battle cries, no grand gestures of fearlessness. The courage leaders need today is subtler, quieter and far more personal.

It shows up when you share an unpopular truth in a tense room. When you admit you don't have all the answers. When you make a decision knowing it won't please everyone. When you open yourself up to judgement, criticism or failure whilst doing what you believe to be right.

Because real courage isn't about being fearless. It's about being willing to be vulnerable.

This is the courage of Graceful Power: daring to do the thing that matters most, even when you feel exposed, uncertain or afraid.

The traditional view of courage

We all think we know what courage looks like, don't we? Being bold, brave, fearless – tackling challenges head-on, no matter the risks. That's the narrative we're often told. But courage in the context of leadership, especially when grounded in Graceful Power, can look and feel very different.

Human beings are storytellers. Through stories, we make sense of the world – learning our society's values and taboos, the threats to avoid and the rewards awaiting those clever, good or bold enough to claim them. From ancient Greek myths to modern blockbusters, we've told tales of heroic warriors who fearlessly pursue their mission. Sometimes they live to tell the tale. Sometimes they don't.

Occasionally, these heroes reveal their inner fear – Achilles hesitates in battle, Indiana Jones recoils at the sight of snakes – but more often than not, we're left with the impression that courage means pushing through without fear, ignoring or overriding any doubts.

The problem is that narrative creates an impossible standard. When leaders believe they're supposed to be fearless, they often mask their uncertainty, hide their doubts and protect themselves behind a polished façade. The irony is that this armour distances them from others. By trying to appear invulnerable, they lose the connection, trust and influence they need most.

Courage is not fearlessness

In truth, courage doesn't arise in the absence of fear. Courage is the decision to act in spite of fear – and often because of it.

Firefighters aren't fearless when they enter a burning building. They're highly trained professionals – deeply aware of the risks. Their courage lies in choosing to act anyway. The same is true for police officers facing danger, doctors making life-saving decisions under pressure, soldiers sweeping unfamiliar terrain or teachers holding their ground in an unruly classroom.

Leaders with Graceful Power aren't fearless either. They don't dismiss risk or discomfort. Instead, they acknowledge fear and treat it as useful information. They recognize the signals it sends – physical, emotional and mental – and use that data to think clearly and choose wisely.

Crucially, they're willing to be open about what they don't know, about where they feel stretched and about the uncertainty they're holding. That vulnerability doesn't undermine their authority; it strengthens it. When leaders are willing to show their humanity, others trust them more deeply – because they see themselves reflected there.

Case study: Anabel Hoult – when courage means letting people in

In early 2020, when the COVID-19 pandemic hit, Anabel Hoult, CEO of Which?, found herself locked down in her North London flat with her husband and two young sons. An outdoorsy, high-energy family, they quickly had to adapt to the new reality of home-schooling and home-working, like millions of others. But Anabel had an additional pressure: she was also leading a national organization, with hundreds of employees looking to her for clarity and confidence during a time of crisis.

It was uncharted territory. She felt as overwhelmed and anxious as anyone – worried for her family, unsure of what lay ahead. How could she lead confidently when she was feeling anything but? How could she offer optimism when she herself felt lost?

Anabel holds herself to high standards. She is both tough and warm, results-driven and deeply compassionate. Until now, she had kept her personal and professional lives carefully separate. But lockdown blurred that boundary completely. In one of our coaching sessions, we explored how to lead authentically from this new reality. She recognized that hiding her own struggle would only widen the gap between her and her people. Though deeply uncomfortable with the idea, she made the courageous decision to let them in.

She turned off her blurred video background, revealing the coat hooks behind her, hung with the everyday mess of family life. Then she began writing daily newsletters to the organization. These updates combined operational clarity with snippets of domestic chaos – honest, humorous, relatable. This vulnerability never became entirely comfortable for Anabel, but it became the bridge that connected her to her team and the feedback was overwhelmingly positive.

Here's an excerpt from her third letter:

> "So, day three of working from home has also been day one of my children being at home. It was a mixed experience – a real treat to have lunch with them and do some craft during a break – but I also had to improve my use of mute in Google Hangouts. Yesterday's lesson? Putting my laptop on a pile of old magazines meant my colleagues could see my face rather than a deeply unflattering view from under my chin!"

As the newsletters continued, something subtle began to shift. People across the organization started replying with their own reflections – tales of interrupted meetings, cabin fever or unexpected moments of joy. Her tone gave others permission to show up more fully and more honestly. It softened interactions, built trust and helped forge a collective resilience that carried the team through the uncertain weeks that followed.

Looking back, Anabel never claimed to enjoy that level of personal exposure. It stretched her, but it also added a new dimension to her leadership. The courage to be real didn't diminish her authority – it deepened her credibility. It allowed others to feel safe in the discomfort of their own realities, because their leader wasn't pretending everything was fine.

Anabel's story shows us that courage isn't about removing fear or pretending to have it all together. Sometimes it's about allowing ourselves to be seen – messy coat hooks and all – and choosing to act even when we feel exposed. For most leaders, that's where courage lives: in the discomfort of vulnerability.

Becoming comfortable with being uncomfortable

The feeling of courage is surprisingly universal. Despite the fear – whether mild or intense – we persuade ourselves to step forward, to quiet the inner noise long enough to act.

This often comes with a cascade of physical sensations as we anticipate the potential threat: a sinking, fluttering or churning in the gut; a sudden loss of appetite; or that rising tightness in the throat that makes swallowing hard. Tension often gathers in the shoulders, forearms and thighs. Meanwhile, the mind races – preoccupied with what could go wrong.

These sensations are your body's way of preparing you for risk. They're a sign that something meaningful is at stake. Recognizing them – and allowing yourself to feel them – is a key part of leading courageously. Suppressing them rarely works. Acknowledging them is an act of courage and vulnerability in itself. This is where the emotional labelling skills we explored in the last chapter – learning to "name it to tame it" – are valuable, helping you bring clarity to moments that might otherwise feel overwhelming.

Yet while the sensation of courage may be common, the act of courage looks very different from person to person. I've worked with leaders who are energized by speaking to a packed auditorium but find emotionally charged one-to-ones deeply uncomfortable – and others who feel the exact opposite. For some, the boldest act of courage is to pause, to not intervene, allowing a situation to unfold. For others, it's stepping in and changing the course someone else has set.

We are all shaped by fear. Our thoughts, behaviours and decisions are influenced – sometimes heavily – by what we find challenging. Yet what we fear varies widely from one person to the next.

Leading with Graceful Power means being courageous enough to identify, examine and accept what feels scary, risky or exposing for you. It's about understanding your own discomfort zones – not what others would find hard, not what theory dictates, but what presses against your edges in the context of your own life and leadership.

Once you've identified those edges, the goal isn't to eliminate fear altogether (though over time, it may soften). The more immediate and realistic aim is to become *comfortable with being uncomfortable.*

Noticing that something feels challenging or exposing is the first step. Choosing to face it anyway – without knowing how it will turn out – that's the courage Graceful Power demands.

Leading with Graceful Power doesn't mean numbing or erasing discomfort. It means feeling it, labelling it and still moving forward. It's about showing up fully, imperfectly and vulnerably – and doing the thing that matters.

This is the essence of courage in Graceful Power: daring to do the things that feel challenging and uncomfortable for you, while allowing yourself to be seen in the process.

Different leaders, different fears

Back in Chapter 5, we explored the importance of purpose and how a team may feel equally committed to a shared goal while being driven by entirely different motivations. The same principle applies to fear. Two people can share the same objective, yet face completely different internal battles to get there.

Following are three anonymized case studies that illustrate some of the most common fears I see holding leaders back from reaching their full potential. We'll revisit these stories over the next two chapters to see how Pritti, Frankie and Philippe each found the courage to push beyond their fears.

Pritti

When she came to coaching, Pritti was in her late 20s and had recently been promoted to a significant regional role. Warm, empathetic and passionate, she excelled at enrolling and energizing the willing. But she was a decade younger than many of the cross-functional peers and local office heads she now needed to influence in order to deliver her projects successfully.

Keenly aware of her youth, Pritti felt uncomfortable taking a firm or challenging stance with those older and more experienced. She either avoided these interactions altogether or overplayed her strengths – becoming excessively enthusiastic in the hope of winning people round. With time, leaning too heavily on this single leadership style began to backfire. What had once been her superpower became a limitation, and her reputation shifted: she came to be seen as an over-excited puppy who lacked the gravitas her role required.

By avoiding the situations that felt most uncomfortable, Pritti gave away her power – and undermined her leadership influence.

Frankie

Frankie was CEO of her thriving start-up in Cape Town when we began working together. Having built the business from scratch, she'd become used to relying entirely on herself – answering every question, solving every challenge, carrying every decision. She had overcome countless obstacles by appearing strong and together, no matter how she was feeling inside.

Now that her business was expanding both locally and internationally, Frankie had a growing team of experts she could trust. Yet she struggled to let anything go. She feared appearing anything less than completely "on it". The idea of showing vulnerability made her deeply uncomfortable – despite longing for greater support and more authentic connection with her team.

By clinging to the leadership style that had built her business – even as the demands changed – she risked becoming the bottleneck to its future growth. Personally, she risked burning out, as she doggedly tried to stay across every detail of a business that had scaled far beyond one person's reach.

Philippe

Philippe had been a trusted stalwart of a software business in Silicon Valley for many years. Loyal to its brilliant and charismatic founder, he had long been a respected team player who role-modelled collaboration and support. As COO, he had helped grow the business while nurturing a strong, inclusive culture.

When the company was bought by a private equity firm and the founder stepped down, Philippe was invited to become CEO. He had the expertise, knowledge and trust of the organization, and his promotion was warmly received by staff who valued his leadership.

But stepping into the limelight proved challenging. In board meetings, Philippe tended to hang back, allowing others to take the lead – a habit that didn't inspire investor confidence. He also put off difficult conversations, whether it was addressing underperformance or cancelling a project. His discomfort with being centre-stage, combined with a deep fear of disappointing others, meant problems often escalated before they were addressed – quietly eroding his impact and credibility.

Discomfort is fear

In all three case studies, the discomfort each leader felt was rooted in fear. They worried certain situations wouldn't go well and doubted they were up to the task of handling them.

In coaching, we explored these fears – deepening their self-awareness, uncovering the strongly held beliefs holding them back and revealing the stories they told themselves about what would happen if they failed. We also paid close attention to the physical discomfort they felt when imagining these scenarios – the racing heart, the tight throat, the churn in the gut – and how those sensations shaped their behaviour. By noticing and labelling these fearful feelings, they became more able to identify what was causing them and how they were responding to them.

Gradually, they started making different choices – not just in action, but in thought. Choosing to think differently helped them feel differently, which, in turn, allowed them to choose new ways forward.

Sometimes it's hard to admit that fear is what's holding us back. We develop strategies to rationalize our behaviour, and over time these patterns become so embedded they're difficult to see – let alone change. Yet these strategies are often the very ways we give away our power.

Even the most outwardly successful leaders can limit their impact by avoiding the conversations, decisions or risks they find most uncomfortable. When asked, they'll usually acknowledge they know the avoidance makes the situation worse – or costs their team or organization something important – yet still find themselves pulled back into the same patterns.

So why do we do it?

To understand that, we need to understand the human fear response – how it has served us and how it often holds us back.

Fear is universal in leadership. It shows up whenever something meaningful is at stake – when you risk your reputation, your relationships or your sense of control. For some, that fear hides behind over-preparation or perfectionism. For others, it shows up as avoidance, people-pleasing or keeping a low profile. However it appears, fear shapes more of our behaviour than most of us realize.

In the next chapter, we'll explore why fear is so potent – how your body and brain respond to threat, how our ancient survival mechanisms play out in modern leadership and how understanding them gives you more freedom to choose. Because the more clearly you understand your fear, the less power it holds over you.

Chapter 8

Understanding fear

For early humans, life was precarious. Survival depended on constant vigilance in a world filled with danger – from predators and harsh environments to rival groups eager to claim scarce resources. Like all animals, we evolved a physiological response to threat: a full-bodied, automatic reaction designed to keep us alive.

This response was essential. A single wrong move could mean injury, illness or death.

At the first sign of danger – the flick of a snake's tail, the scent of wildfire smoke, the sudden rustle of movement in the trees – the brain leapt into action, triggering a cascade of physical changes to prepare the body for survival. Within seconds, energy, focus and awareness heightened, priming our ancestors to:

- **Freeze:** Staying perfectly still and hoping the snake would slither away.
- **Flee:** Outrunning the approaching fire.
- **Fight:** Defending themselves from whatever lurked in the trees.

What we now call "fear" is the bodily experience of this ancient survival system springing into action – a set of automatic, finely tuned reactions designed to maximize our chances of staying alive.

Physiology of the fear response

Think of a time when someone mischievous leapt out to make you jump. There was no real danger – yet your body reacted instantly: your hands shot up, your breath caught, your heart pounded. All of this happened before your conscious mind had even worked out what was happening.

This is our ancient fear response in action – lightning fast, automatic and indiscriminate.

Deep inside the brain, the amygdala, the hypothalamus and the prefrontal cortex work together to detect threat and switch the body from calm to high alert. The hypothalamus signals the adrenal glands to release a surge of adrenaline, setting off a chain reaction:

- Heart rate and blood pressure rise, pumping oxygen and nutrients to muscles and vital organs.
- Blood is redirected away from less critical systems – draining from the face and fingers (causing cold hands or tingling) and slowing digestion (leading to butterflies, dry mouth or difficulty swallowing).
- Breathing becomes faster and shallower, boosting oxygen delivery and helping expel carbon dioxide to fuel rapid action.
- Glucose is released from the liver, providing a burst of energy that can cause trembling.
- Muscles tense – especially in the thighs, arms, shoulders and core – readying the body to run or defend itself.
- Pupils dilate, sharpening vision and heightening awareness of the surroundings.

In seconds, the body is transformed into a finely tuned survival machine – primed and ready to face whatever comes next.

The cognitive revolution: A new kind of fear

For more than a million years, this ancient system served us well. Then, around 70,000 years ago, something remarkable happened: during a period known as the Cognitive Revolution, humans developed a new superpower – the ability to imagine the future, construct stories and share beliefs across the group.

This changed the nature of fear forever.

We were no longer limited to reacting to threats in the moment. We could now anticipate danger – seeing it coming long before it arrived. Humans could warn each other about specific, immediate threats ("There's a group of lions at the bend in the river") and also about potential threats ("This is the time of year lions often come to the river, so take extra care").

Fear evolved from a reflex into a planning tool – helping early humans avoid danger before it struck. We learned to:

- Carry tools in case of attack.
- Stick to safer paths.
- Form cooperative groups to share knowledge, resources and protection.

Living in groups became a huge survival advantage. Together, we could hunt more effectively, defend ourselves more successfully and pass down learning across generations. But there was a trade-off: belonging became critical.

To be excluded from the group – to lose its protection – meant exposure, vulnerability, and, often, death. Over thousands of generations, our brains became exquisitely attuned to the risks of rejection. It didn't stop there. Status within the group also mattered. Higher-status individuals typically had better access to food, shelter and mates, increasing their chances of survival and reproduction.

Suddenly, our deepest fears were no longer just about predators and wildfires. They also became about acceptance and standing – belonging to the group, being valued within it and avoiding the devastating consequences of exclusion or humiliation.

For our earliest ancestors, both rejection and loss of status were genuine existential threats – and those ancient instincts still live within us today.

The evolution of the fear response

So, in the 70,000 years since the Cognitive Revolution transformed human thinking, how has our fear response evolved to distinguish between actual, immediate threats and possible, future ones? Not at all.

Our bodies react in exactly the same way to a predator in the wild as they do to a tense conversation tomorrow, or even a completely imagined danger that will never happen.

In the past 24 hours alone, my own body has jolted into high alert in response to:

- A dispute with our water supplier, who was threatening to significantly overcharge.
- Our dog barking unexpectedly late at night.
- The shocking opening episode of a drama based on the bombing of Pan Am Flight 103 over Lockerbie in 1988.
- Driving on untreated, icy roads in –7°C temperatures.

Four very different situations. One identical physiological response: a surge of adrenaline, a racing heart, tense muscles, faster breathing. The body doesn't stop to ask whether the threat is life-or-death or entirely imagined – it simply reacts.

Your body reacts: Your mind interprets

Let's test this for yourself.

Imagine being in an environment that makes you anxious:

- Standing on the edge of a cliff if you're afraid of heights.
- Stuck in a lift if you dislike confined spaces.
- Swimming in the middle of a deep, dark lake if open water unsettles you.
- Walking alone and lost through a forest after dark.

Pause for a moment, close your eyes and visualize yourself there. Allow yourself to feel the unease building. Notice the subtle stirrings in your body – your heartbeat picking up, the muscles in your shoulders tightening, your breath shallowing slightly.

Now, try a different scenario: imagine a social situation you'd find uncomfortable:

- A networking event where you'll need to make small talk with strangers.
- A wedding or funeral where you've been asked to give a speech.
- A school reunion with people you haven't seen for decades.

Close your eyes and picture yourself there. Let the awkwardness rise just enough to feel it. Can you sense the faint flutter of adrenaline? The churn in your gut? Perhaps even a tightening in your chest?

These are entirely imaginary situations. I'm not about to send you into any of them. So, the physical response is mild. Yet, you may have noticed something interesting: your mind getting busy. You might have felt the beginnings of an inner dialogue – a drive to prepare, an urge to avoid or perhaps a quiet shutting down to escape the discomforting scenario.

Now, if these scenarios were actually about to happen this weekend. Your anxiety levels would rise a little higher.

Then, if you suddenly found yourself right there – toes on the cliff edge or microphone in hand before a sea of expectant faces – the intensity of your body's response would escalate again.

Yet across all these versions – imagined, anticipated and immediate – your body still produces the same automatic fear response. The intensity may dial up or down depending on how "real" the danger feels, but the underlying mechanism doesn't change.

The mind's storytelling trap

Here's where it gets even more fascinating, and more relevant to leadership.

Your body may only have one physical fear response, but your mind can weave an infinite number of stories around it. A single rush of adrenaline can become:

- "I'm nervous."
- "I'm under pressure."
- "I'm failing."
- "I'm unsafe."
- "I don't belong here."

Same biology. Completely different narratives.

Those narratives shape far more than how you feel. They influence the meaning you give an event, the choices you make in response, and ultimately, the behaviours you adopt as a leader.

- A skipping heartbeat before presenting to the board can become: "I'm excited and ready." Or it can become: "I'm going to embarrass myself."
- A colleague's frown can mean: "They're stressed about something." Or: "They think I've failed."
- That inner flutter before a big decision can signal: "This matters and I'm focused." Or: "I'm out of my depth."

When we fail to notice the difference between the body's automatic response and the story the mind builds around it, we give our fears far more power than they deserve.

This distinction is at the heart of courageous leadership: learning to recognize the story you're telling yourself and choosing whether to keep it, rewrite it or let it go.

The safety vs status paradox for leaders

Perhaps the ultimate paradox of leadership is this: our most primitive desire to feel safe and accepted within the group is in direct tension with our equally powerful drive for status, autonomy and distinction.

Both are deep, universal needs – each with strong biological and evolutionary roots.

Being accepted keeps us safe. Fitting in brings reassurance and belonging. For our ancestors, safety within the tribe meant survival. At the same time, higher status brought access to better resources, greater influence and more opportunities for us and our descendants – improving our chances of long-term success.

This same tension plays out in leadership today. We must learn to navigate the ancient, conflicting impulses still operating within us – the need for social safety and the hunger for status. This tension doesn't diminish with seniority. In fact, the stakes – and the psychological load – often increase.

Why status feels like survival

Recent neuroscience offers insight into why leadership so often feels personally exposing. David Rock's[1] research into the social brain shows that the human brain processes threats to our social standing, belonging or influence in much the same way it processes threats to physical safety.

When our sense of acceptance, competence or status feels at risk, the same threat-detection systems in the brain – especially the amygdala – fire as if we were facing a predator. The surge of adrenaline, the rapid heartbeat, the muscle tension – all are triggered automatically, even when the "danger" is entirely social.

This explains why seemingly everyday leadership challenges – giving tough feedback, making an unpopular decision, admitting you don't have all the answers or risking visible failure – can feel so personally threatening. Our conscious minds may understand it's not life-or-death, but our bodies still react as though it is.

That's why even senior, highly capable leaders often describe:

- A reluctance to speak up in certain environments.
- A powerful need to impress and "earn their place".
- Anxiety around giving feedback or making unpopular calls.

These reactions aren't weaknesses. They're ancient survival mechanisms playing out in modern contexts. Recognizing this link – and learning to work with it – is critical to leading with courage today.

The value and cost of the fear response today

Our fear response still serves us well – occasionally in exactly the same way it did for our ancestors. When we face genuine physical danger – a growling dog, a car unexpectedly breaking sharply on the road in front of us, a child choking on food – the sharpened senses, heightened focus and physical readiness it triggers can be lifesaving.

But for most of us, true life-or-death situations are rare. Our environments are increasingly designed to protect us: seatbelts, safety standards, vaccinations, health and safety regulations and warning systems minimize daily physical risk.

And yet, our ancient life-protection system is triggered constantly – not by wild predators but by abstract, conceptual threats.

We live amid a constant background hum of:

- 24-hour news cycles filled with crises and catastrophe.
- Social media fuelling comparison, status anxiety and self-doubt.
- Divisive political discourse that leaves us feeling under siege.
- War, famine, and shifting geopolitics feeding a sense of global fragility and unease.

These situations aren't immediately physically dangerous, but your brain can interpret them as threats – and your body reacts as if your survival is at stake.

For leaders, these triggers are amplified. Modern leadership demands a daily balancing act: boldness versus caution, innovation versus stability, risk versus reward. The fear of "getting it wrong" runs alongside the exhilaration of breaking new ground.

Today, our ancient fear response often works against us. In a world where most threats aren't life-or-death, unmanaged fear can limit our thinking, drain our confidence and hold us back as leaders. When left unchecked, fear can:

- Narrow your thinking and reduce your capacity to see creative solutions.
- Make you defensive, reactive or hesitant when boldness is required.
- Quietly erode confidence, connection and clarity of purpose.

Fear, when understood, can be a source of focus and energy. But when ignored or suppressed, it can quietly run your leadership – shaping your choices without your awareness and keeping you smaller than you intend to be.

Viewing fear differently: Pachad and norah

In his book *Be Still and Get Going*,[2] Alan Lew explains that the Hebrew Bible uses two distinct words for fear: Pachad and norah.

This ancient distinction is surprisingly useful for modern leaders. These two kinds of fear feel different, arise from different sources and require different responses.

Pachad: Fear of imagined threat

- The dread we feel when projecting into the future and imagining what could go wrong.
- An over-reactive, often irrational fear rooted in perceived danger rather than real risk.
- A warning signal, sometimes accurate, but often exaggerated.

Norah: Fear in the presence of expansion

- The sensation we experience when we're stepping into something bigger than we've known before.

- A sudden surge of energy that accompanies growth, visibility or greater responsibility.
- A sense of awe and aliveness, the tingling awareness of possibility and potential.

To put it simply: Pachad is the anxiety you feel before giving a big speech, imagining everything that might go wrong. Norah is the thrill you feel during the speech, realizing you're rising to the moment.

Why this distinction matters for leaders

When building courage for Graceful Power, pachad and norah play different roles:

- Pachad needs to be acknowledged. It can highlight genuine risks or areas that require care. But it also needs to be quietened, so it doesn't keep you small, cautious or stuck.
- Norah, on the other hand, is to be embraced. It signals you are expanding – stepping into new territory, stretching your capacity and living closer to your potential.

Pachad has value. It keeps us safe from recklessness, reins in blind optimism and reminds us to weigh consequences thoughtfully. But when left unchecked, pachad fuels worst-case-scenario thinking, erodes self-trust and narrows our leadership presence. It keeps us second-guessing ourselves just when clarity and courage are most needed.

Norah feels different. It is the aliveness that comes when we lead more boldly, speak more honestly or stand more visibly in our power. It's what arises when we dare to take up more space, knowing there is no guarantee of success.

Rabbi Lew describes norah as:

> "The sudden and frightening eruption of a new strength, the feeling that we are possessed of far more energy than we can handle, that our reality is not as bounded as we thought, but

> frighteningly boundless... that our life is far more intense than we imagined, that we are far more powerful, and far more vulnerable to loss, than we supposed."

Norah is awe-inspiring and nerve-wracking all at once. It reveals our greater potential – and our greater vulnerability. Sometimes, we fear living fully as much as we fear failure. Choosing the smaller, safer path can feel easier than risking the pain of failing to achieve something that truly matters.

To lead with Graceful Power, we need both. Pachad keeps us grounded, thoughtful and measured. But we also need to recognize, accept – and at times lean into – the fear of norah. It's the signal we're growing, stretching beyond our comfort zone and stepping into the space our potential is asking us to inhabit.

The resistance that comes with growth

When we're called to expand, it rarely feels comfortable. Norah carries energy and possibility, but alongside it comes resistance – often disguised as perfectly reasonable thoughts and feelings:

- **Lack of self-belief:** "Who am I to take on this role?"
- **Doubting our abilities:** "Someone more skilled or experienced will do this better than me."
- **Fear of rejection or losing face:** "I'll look foolish." "People won't like me for this."
- **Failure to see our uniqueness:** "Someone else will already be doing this."
- **Rationalizing staying small:** "I'm doing fine as I am. I'm busy, valued and successful enough."

These are deeply human responses. But they are also the very places where we start giving away our power. When we misread our fear of growth as a sign we're not ready – we risk shrinking back from the opportunities where we're being called to lead.

Bungee jumping: A metaphor for expansion

In my twenties, while backpacking in Australia, I became unexpectedly enthralled by bungee jumping. At first, I had no intention of trying it myself. Two fellow travellers, Greg and Chris, were planning to jump, and I volunteered to hold their valuables, thinking the whole thing was a rather silly idea.

We arrived at the site on the Queensland coast and watched the jumpers ascend the 50-metre platform. After the bungee cord was strapped to their ankles, each one leapt on the count of three. Some were silent; most were not. But every single one landed grinning, whooping, fist-pumping – utterly exhilarated.

For Greg and Chris, the anticipation had caused a sleepless night. I, on the other hand, had been calm. I wasn't jumping. But watching the joy of the jumpers changed something in me. Greg grew more anxious, Chris quietly decided against jumping at all – and I suddenly found myself thinking: "I want what they're having."

Before I knew it, I'd signed up.

As my ankles were bound, a member of the jump team pointed to a white house perched on a distant cliff and told me to dive towards it. In that instant, two contradictory thoughts collided: "I'm going to die!" – a shrinking, terrified feeling; "I'm going to fly!" – a surging, expansive thrill. I chose to jump.

And, for just a moment, I flew. Even now, decades later, I can still feel it: the warm wind on my face, the white house on the horizon, the breathtaking weightlessness. Then came the fall, the scream, the bounce – and finally, the laughter. Greg and I laughed ecstatically for the rest of the day. I suspect Chris may have regretted his decision, just a little.

That moment on the platform – suspended between what could go wrong and what could go right – was an exquisite collision of pachad and norah. Pachad whispered of danger and failure; norah pulled me towards possibility and expansion. That day, I chose norah. And I'm grateful I did.

Now pause for a moment and think about a time when you stood on your own "platform" – facing a situation that carried both risk and possibility. It might have been giving a presentation, applying for a promotion, speaking up in a meeting, starting a business or having a difficult conversation that mattered deeply. Can you remember the collision of feelings – the tightening of pachad warning you of what might go wrong, and the surge of norah calling you towards something bigger? Remember what you chose in that moment. Did you step forward or step back? How did it feel – in your body, your mind, your heart – to make that choice? Given the situation again, would you make the same choice or a different one?

Where fear holds your leadership back

Let's return to the three leaders we met earlier in Chapter 7: Pritti, Frankie and Philippe.

- Pritti avoided taking a firm stance with senior colleagues.
- Frankie refused to loosen her grip on every detail.
- Philippe stayed in the shadows, reluctant to step into visible leadership.

Each of them gave away their power – not because they lacked ability, but because fear was running the show. Past experiences, self-doubt and imagined worst-case scenarios had triggered their body's fear response. Rather than leaning into the discomfort of norah – stepping into growth – they unconsciously chose pachad's safety instead:

- Pritti turned up the enthusiasm, hoping to win people over rather than challenging them.
- Frankie doubled down on control, keeping her team at arm's length.
- Philippe continued to let others take the spotlight, avoiding the exposure of visible leadership.

Each of these leaders faced their own version of standing on the platform – suspended between the safety of the familiar and the risk of stepping into something bigger. Their stories are different, but the pattern is universal. Fear whispers to all of us in leadership: "Play it safe. Stay where you are. Don't risk getting it wrong."

Sometimes that's wise – pachad is doing its job, keeping us cautious where caution is warranted. But other times, that same voice is holding us back from norah – the energy, possibility and growth waiting on the other side of discomfort.

This is where reflection becomes powerful. By looking at your own patterns through this new lens, you can start to see where fear might be shaping your choices – and where you have the opportunity to choose differently.

Now, it's your turn to experiment with the following structured reflection exercise.

Exercise: Reframing fear

Step 1: Spot the fear

Think about an aspect of your leadership role where you've felt resistance, avoidance or self-doubt.

- Where do you find yourself holding back or playing small?
- What situation do you dread, delay or overprepare for?
- What feedback have you received that points towards an area of growth you haven't yet stepped into?

Write down one or two situations that come to mind.

Step 2: Name the story

For each situation, ask yourself:

- "What am I afraid might happen?"
- "What's the worst story my mind is telling me here?"

Remember, your body's fear response only knows threat – it doesn't distinguish between a genuine danger and an imagined one. Identifying the story gives you space to question it.

Step 3: Pachad or norah?

Now, reflect on whether what you're feeling is pachad or norah:

- If it's pachad, your fear is projecting imagined future dangers – rejection, failure, embarrassment – and trying to keep you "safe" by holding you back.
- If it's norah, you're on the edge of expansion – stretching into a bigger version of yourself, which naturally feels risky but carries possibility and growth.

Step 4: Reframe possibility

Choose one situation and rewrite your story:

- If you leaned into the discomfort, what could become possible?
- How might your leadership, your influence or your impact expand?
- What would choosing norah look like in this moment?

Step 5: Lead yourself

Imagine you're coaching someone else through this exact situation.

- What would you say to them?
- How would you help them see that fear is dictating their behaviour?
- How would you inspire them with a vision of what could open up if they stepped forward?

Now turn that same advice inward. What do you need to hear from yourself? How might this reflection and reframe shape your behaviour going forward?

The trap of "that's just who I am"

I've noticed a common tendency – even among the most accomplished leaders – for people to let themselves off the hook of growth by claiming fear-driven behaviour as part of their identity. With a resigned shrug, they say: "I'm impatient"; "I'm a perfectionist"; "I'm not good with people"; "I've always had a quick temper".

It feels harmless, even self-aware – but it quietly relieves us of the responsibility of facing into the discomfort of change.

The truth is these aren't fixed traits. They're learned patterns – behaviours shaped by experience, repetition and reinforcement. They may once have served us. They may even still serve us in certain contexts. But over time, they can start to limit us if we accept them as permanent truths.

Years ago, I coached a CEO we'll call Steve. Known for being successful but blunt and bullish, he had a reputation for losing his temper. He was infamous for shouting at his team and driving performance through fear. I'll admit I was nervous before our first meeting. But what I found wasn't a tyrant – it was a man trapped by his own habits.

He hated who he'd become, yet he feared that changing would make him ineffective: "This is who I am. I don't know how to be anything else. If I stop acting like this, I've no idea how to drive success."

It took courage for Steve to see that he didn't need to become someone else – he needed to become even more fully of himself. His ability to be bold, to challenge and to demand high standards was a strength. But he needed more than just a hammer in his leadership toolbox.

A skilled tradesperson doesn't use a hammer for every problem, and neither should a leader. Expanding your leadership means choosing different tools – even when they feel clumsy or unfamiliar at first.

A simple shift: "Until now..."

One of the most liberating phrases I teach my clients is: "Until now..."

"Until now..." creates a pause. It acknowledges who you've been while opening the door to who you're becoming. It reminds you that you always have choice.

- Until now, I wasn't confident giving praise. I'm now practising and improving.
- Until now, I let others take the lead. From now on I'm choosing to step forward more often.
- Until now, I avoided networking events. I'm now engaging with one or two people each time.
- Until now, I believed being "in the detail" kept me safe. Now I practise letting go.

"Until now..." separates your past from your future. It names your fear, honours your growth and returns you to your power.

Because the truth is: you don't need to be fearless to lead. You simply need to be willing to meet your fear – gracefully, powerfully and one step at a time.

Returning to your power

This is a passage from Marianne Williamson's *A Return to Love*[3] that I've shared with many clients over the years.

> "Our deepest fear is not that we are inadequate. Our deepest fear is that we are powerful beyond measure. It is our light, not our darkness, that most frightens us. We ask ourselves, 'Who am I to be brilliant, gorgeous, talented, fabulous?' Actually, who are you not to be?... Your playing small does not serve the world. There's nothing enlightened about shrinking so that other people won't feel insecure around you. We are all meant to shine as children do... And as we let our light shine, we

unconsciously give other people permission to do the same. As we're liberated from our own fear, our presence automatically liberates others."

In challenging times, when fear is pervasive, we need leaders willing to stand fully in their power – not by pretending to be fearless, but by courageously choosing to show up and shine their light as their whole, human selves.

Exercise: Shining your light

As we close this chapter, take a few minutes to imagine what it would be like to fully shine your light – to courageously step into this liberated version of yourself.

Take out your notebook and pen, then set a timer for 10 minutes. Let your thoughts flow freely onto the page – no editing, no judgment, no holding back.

Reflect on these prompts:

- What would be the most thrilling act of expansion for you right now?
- What aspect of yourself are you secretly yearning to reveal?
- What is your undervalued strength – the "superpower" the world would benefit from if you let it shine?
- If you knew you couldn't fail, what would you liberate yourself to achieve?
- If you were to take just one small step towards this act of expansion today, what would it be?

When you finish writing, pause and reflect. Let you answers land and feel the thrill and the fear of what could be possible for you.

Now, take that first step – however small, because this is how courage builds: one step at a time.

Fear isn't a sign of weakness – it's a deeply human response, designed to keep us safe. In this chapter, we've explored where fear comes from, how it shows up in your body and mind, and why it so often drives your leadership choices without you realizing it.

The goal isn't to eliminate fear, but to understand it – to recognize when it's useful and when it's holding you back from growth, possibility and impact.

In the next chapter, we'll take this understanding further. You'll learn practical techniques to manage your fear more skilfully and unlock the steady courage beneath.

Chapter 9

Managing fear and unlocking courage

Fear isn't something to be conquered or eliminated. It's an essential part of being human – one of the most important forces shaping our growth, our relationships and our leadership. Far from being a sign of weakness, fear can be evidence that you're standing on the edge of possibility and expansion.

Leaders who demonstrate the courage needed for Graceful Power haven't eliminated fear, nor do they ignore it. Instead, they see it as a source of valuable information rather than something that dictates their behaviour. They've learnt to accept the safety-first bias of our primitive brain and its triggering of pachad. They continue to stretch beyond their comfort zones, leaning into norah as they explore their full capabilities.

Heightening awareness and acceptance of fearful thoughts

To harness fear so it supports your growth rather than stifles it, you first need to become highly attuned to it. That means being able to articulate what you are afraid of and why. The hardest – and most liberating – shift you can make is to accept your fears without judgement. Not to decide whether they're rational or irrational, valid or invalid, but simply to acknowledge: "These fears are real for me."

Then the space opens for you to choose how to respond to the information they bring, rather than simply reacting to the potential risk.

The exercises in this chapter will guide you to do just that. They may ask you to lean into thoughts you usually try to avoid. This might be new and uncomfortable territory for you. You may notice the body's natural fear responses kicking in – shoulders tightening, breath shortening, your heart beating quicker or a sinking sensation in your stomach. These are signals: your body telling you that you've touched on something significant.

Sometimes the physical sensations arrive before the fearful thought and associated emotions; sometimes the thoughts trigger the feelings. Either way, they feed one another in a reinforcing loop.

This cycle is natural – and, crucially, it can be interrupted.

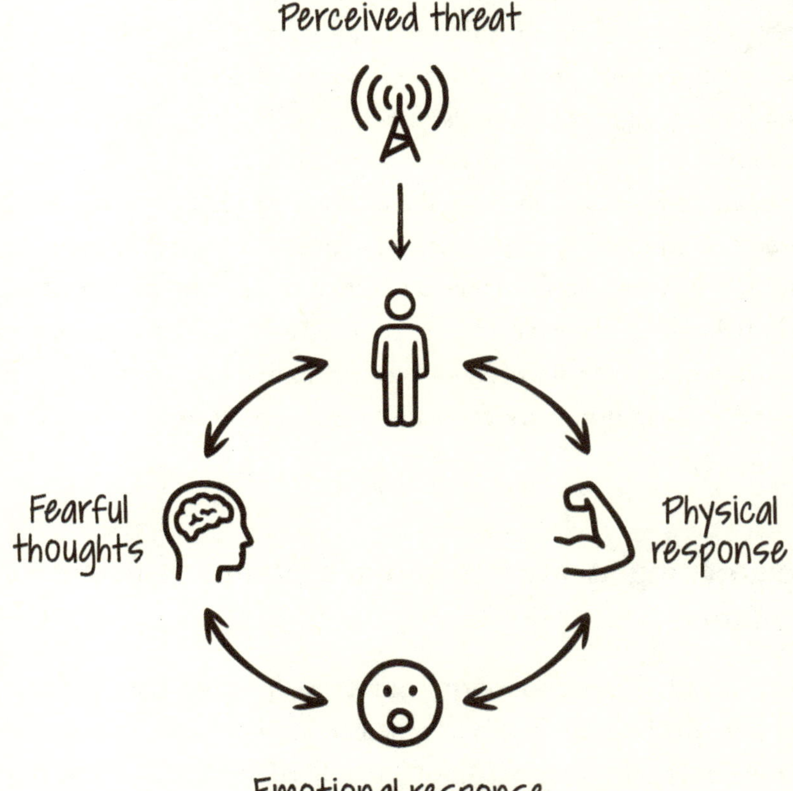

Externalize and characterize your fears

One effective technique to interrupt this loop is to externalize the fearful thoughts. To imagine these are not your thoughts, but the voices of external characters. These voices may only be audible to you, but they are not *you*.

This separation creates space – enough distance for you to observe, question and ultimately manage these voices rather than being ruled by them. Over the coming pages, you'll begin to meet your personal cast of fear-driven characters and practise strategies to reclaim the space they've been occupying – so that your inner voice of wisdom becomes louder and clearer, making courageous choices easier.

Two fearful tribes: Alarmists and Trolls

Within each of us live two distinct "tribes", both devoted to keeping us safe, but using very different tactics. Together, they weave a web of anxiety designed to keep us safely within our comfort zone and steering us away from the vulnerability that always accompanies growth.

The Alarmists

Imagine a tribe of meerkat-like creatures: twitchy, hyper-alert, constantly scanning the horizon. These are the Alarmists – your internal sentries. Their job is simple: spot danger and raise the alarm.

They are the catastrophizers, the "everything-will-go-wrong" messengers. They thrive on exaggeration, knowing the drama grabs your attention, and so they turn up the volume.

Their warnings sound urgent and their energy is contagious. They have a direct line to your fight-or-flight response and are quick to hit the panic button. Left unchecked, they'll keep you on permanent high alert too, exhausting your emotional and physical reserves.

The Trolls

If the Alarmists trade in anxiety, the Trolls trade in shame. They don't warn you that *something* will go wrong – they whisper that *you* are what's wrong.

Their tactics are quieter but more insidious: undermining your confidence, replaying past failures, questioning your adequacy and subtly persuading you not to try. Their intention is protective – they want to keep you safe from failure, humiliation or rejection – but their effect is paralyzing.

I've chosen to call them "Trolls" because, like their online namesakes, they hide in the shadows, emboldened by anonymity to say unspeakable things they would never dare voice in daylight. You may have heard them called "inner critics", "saboteurs" or "gremlins" before. Whatever the name, the function is the same: they undermine you to deter you from stepping into perceived danger.

Alarmists vs Trolls

Alarmists	**Trolls**
Shout: "Everything will go wrong!"	Whisper: "You're not good enough."
Trigger anxiety and hyper-vigilance	Trigger shame and self-doubt
Use panic and overreaction	Use belittling and criticism
Goal: Keep you out of harm's way	Goal: Stop you from trying at all

Both tribes believe they're protecting you. In reality, they're keeping you from growth. While keeping you safe they are also keeping you small.

The good news? Once you've identified these voices and understood their tactics, you can begin to manage them differently. Doing so requires two distinct strategies – one for the Alarmists, one for the Trolls.

CALMING THE ALARMISTS

The Alarmist tribe mean well – they really do. They've been charged with keeping you safe from threats, real or imagined, and they take their job seriously. Their constant vigilance alerts you to the pitfalls and failures that *might* lie ahead. They warn you against trying a bold new haircut, asking for a pay rise, applying for a new role or changing your life entirely. Sometimes, the information they offer is genuinely useful – occasionally even essential.

The challenge is that every time the Alarmists share one of their risk assessments, they trigger your fear response, plunging you into fight, flight or freeze:

- **Fight:** Defending yourself through overly assertive or aggressive behaviour.
- **Flight:** Avoiding the situation entirely.
- **Freeze:** Overthinking, procrastinating or becoming paralyzed.

Spectrum of all possible outcomes

The trick to calming the fearful feelings created by the danger-focused Alarmists is to recognize that they're tuned into only one end of the *spectrum of all possible outcomes*.

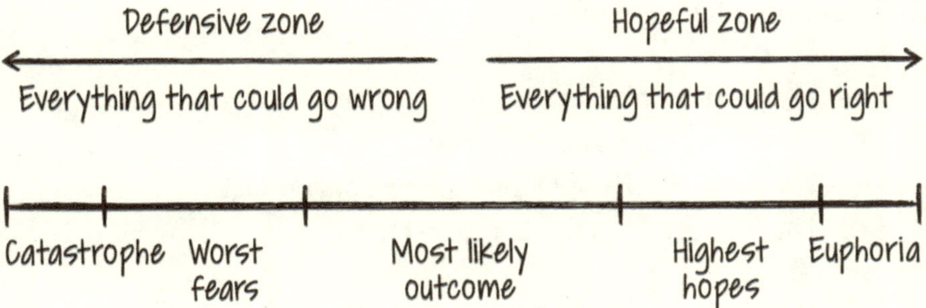

This spectrum stretches from *everything that could go wrong* at one extreme to *everything that could go right* at the other. The Alarmists are true pessimists: incapable of seeing the most likely outcomes and completely uninterested in what could go well.

Whenever you're anticipating a big event, a difficult conversation or a new venture – anything that pushes you beyond your comfort zone – it's vital to consider the *full spectrum* of possibilities.

If your perspective is dictated by the Alarmists' fearful voices, your instinct will be to play safe. That may help you avoid catastrophe, but it also narrows your vision, restricts creativity and limits your potential.

By contrast, when you adopt a balanced, full-spectrum mindset – one that acknowledges risk *and* embraces opportunity – your decisions become braver, more hopeful and far more creative.

Case study: Caged by limiting belief

Christina had built a strong reputation as an expert within her organizational function. It was time to broaden her influence and position herself as her boss's successor by leading a high-profile cross-functional project. She and her boss agreed this was her opportunity to showcase her leadership and expand her reach beyond her immediate expertise. Six months later, nothing had happened.

In coaching, it became clear that Christina's Alarmists were in charge. She was stuck in procrastination – analysing, doubting, avoiding. So, I asked her to sketch the *spectrum of all possible outcomes* and start by listing her *worst fears*:

- My peers won't engage with my plans.
- I won't make enough progress.
- They'll think the outcomes aren't bold enough.
- The initiative will fail completely.

Then, I took her into the *catastrophe* zone by asking "And what would happen then?". She paused, then continued:

- Everyone will think I'm useless.
- I'll be fired and leave in shame.

- My reputation will be ruined.
- I'll never work again.

As she spoke these last fears aloud, she began to laugh. "I *know* these won't actually happen, but the panicked voice in me whispers that they could."

Simply articulating her fears – and naming them as the voice of her Alarmists – gave her distance from them. It created space for her wiser, grounded voice to emerge.

From there, we moved focus to the other end of the spectrum. I dared her to be optimistic, to explore her *highest hopes*:

- I'll be seen as someone who gets things done.
- I'll be recognized as the natural successor to my boss.
- My boss will feel confident taking his next step.

I pushed her even further: "If these are your highest hopes, what's the euphoric outcome beyond them?" Christina grinned: "I'll be promoted to President, fast-tracked to CEO, and given a huge bonus!"

In that moment, she shifted from frozen to energized. She realized that a long-standing belief, "I can't share an opinion unless I'm the expert", had once served her, but her Alarmists had turned it into a cage.

Before, she had been standing on the spectrum with her attention fixed firmly on the left – the world of potential failure. Once she turned to face what could go right, her whole mindset changed, and with it her energy. She reconnected with her adjacent strengths: curiosity, strong relationships, good judgement, strategic thinking. Expertise was valuable, but it wasn't the only quality she brought.

From this balanced place, she planned forward – focusing on who she needed to *be* to make her *highest hopes* the more likely outcome: "Curious and collaborative with all stakeholders, motivating everyone to build a shared vision."

Balancing awareness of risk with hopeful intention, Christina stepped into action.

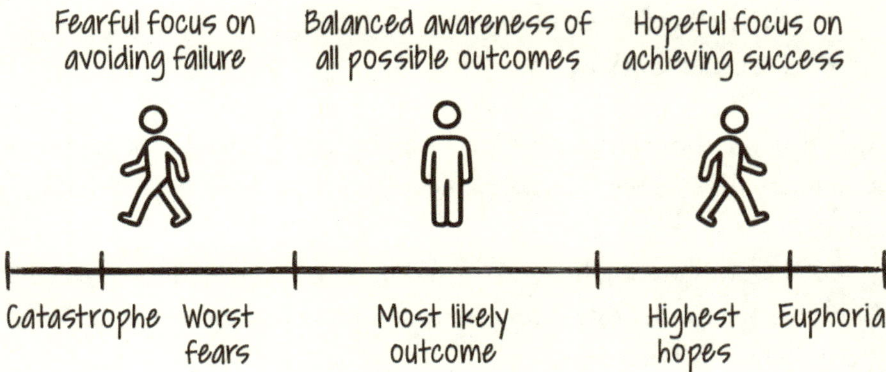

Why imagine both catastrophe and euphoria?

Why is it so important to articulate both the *catastrophic* and *euphoric* ends of the spectrum? Because these extremes are powerful emotional drivers – and when they remain unspoken, they quietly shape our decisions and behaviours without us realizing.

Many people resist talking about these extremes because they're emotionally loaded. Catastrophe can feel paralyzing. Euphoria can feel unrealistic or self-indulgent. Yet both are possible – unlikely, yes, but *possible* – and naming them is liberating.

Speaking your very worst fears aloud reduces their power. Voicing your most hopeful, thrilling ambitions expands your perspective and motivation. This is the territory of pachad and norah: when you consciously face both the imagined disaster and the glorious success, you give yourself more agency over your choices.

As the saying goes: "Shoot for the moon. Even if you miss, you'll land among the stars."

Case study: Blind optimism

Jack and Gamba, best friends turned business partners, had left secure jobs to launch a bold new venture. They were confident, energized and aligned in their vision.

During a coaching session, I asked them how they planned to handle conflict between them or navigate the inevitable setbacks along the way. Gamba's face went blank. Jack looked stunned.

In their shared vision, there was no room for conflict, failure or challenge. The culture they were building only allowed space for success. Any thought of things going wrong felt almost like betrayal.

This presents its own challenge: if you can't acknowledge what might go wrong, you can't prepare for it. Jack and Gamba were standing at the *highest hopes* end of the spectrum, facing only their imagined best-case future. They risked being blindsided and demoralized at the first significant hurdle.

Through coaching, they bravely turned to face the uncomfortable possibility of failure and began designing their working relationship as intentionally as their business strategy:

- Discussing potential sources of conflict.
- Agreeing how they would communicate and support each other.
- Committing to flag early warning signs before resentment could build.

They launched without their earlier blind optimism and instead with a shared plan to stay aligned – through the challenges as well as the successes.

Courageous leadership requires full-spectrum vision

Sometimes, courage means daring to look away from everything that could go wrong. Other times, it means daring to look away from everything that could go right.

Courage in Graceful Power is about acknowledging the *full spectrum* – then orienting yourself toward the outcomes you want to make more likely. It's not about ignoring risk, but it's not about being ruled by it either.

It's about choosing to lead hopefully, not defensively.

Exercise: Practising full-spectrum vision

Choose a course of action you've been considering – perhaps something you've been putting off, or something already underway that makes you feel anxious or exposed. Ideally, pick a situation that stretches you: something that makes your pulse quicken or your stomach churn when you think about it. It could be as significant as changing careers, or as everyday as giving feedback to a team member or challenging someone's opinion in a meeting.

Tip: Pick something that's taking up more of your mental bandwidth than it deserves.

Step 1: Create your spectrum

Make a physical version of the spectrum of all possible outcomes:

- Draw it on paper.
- Map it across a table using objects.
- Or, best of all, lay it out across the floor of a room. Use anything you have to hand – books, cushions, mugs, pens – to mark the key points: worst fears to catastrophe, highest hopes to euphoria.

Step 2: Move through the spectrum

Hold your chosen action clearly in mind and walk through each point step by step, repositioning yourself appropriately:

- **Worst fears:** Give your Alarmists full permission to speak. What could go wrong? Notice your thoughts, feelings and physical sensations.
- **Catastrophe:** Ask yourself, "And then what would happen?" Push your Alarmists to the very edge of disaster. Jot down notes to neutralize their power.
- **Pause and reset:** Take a few slow breaths, shake out your arms and release tension before shifting your focus.

- **Highest hopes:** Stand taller, breathe deeper and imagine everything going right. Let the norah rise – the thrill of possibility.
- **Euphoria:** Go big. Imagine the wildest success you can. Smile at its audacity. Enjoy it.

Step 3: Centre yourself

Now, stand at the midpoint of the spectrum – grounded between pachad and norah – and ask yourself:

- Which part of the spectrum have I been standing in most often?
- What have I been avoiding?
- What would change if I focused more on hopeful outcomes?
- What risks can I mitigate with better planning?
- How would I act if I led with courage, not defensiveness?

Make a note of your answers, then take a step back and consider what you have learnt during this exercise. Now make a plan for how things will be different going forward.

TAMING YOUR TROLLS

Now that your Alarmists are playing a healthier role – helping you assess risks rather than dominate your decisions – it's time to meet the darker voices in your personal safety team: your tribe of Trolls.

Working alongside the Alarmists and their focus on *what* might go wrong, the Trolls specialize in something more personal: a steady stream of judgement about how *you* are wrong.

It can be confronting – even painful – to identify and separate the Trolls' narrative from your wiser thoughts. That's why we need to create distance between *you* and *them*. Trolls may speak directly to you and about you, but they are *not* you. Once you learn to recognize them, you can choose whether or not to listen.

This takes a little imagination – and a little playfulness. Playfulness, in fact, is one of the most effective tools for taming Trolls. One of the best ways to weaken their grip is simply to stop taking them so seriously.

So, as we explore how to recognize and manage your Trolls, picture them vividly: strange, ugly, slightly comical creatures squatting nearby, hissing and spitting their mean little words – but very definitely separate from you. Imagine them now, perched on the arm of the sofa, the bookshelf or the window ledge across the room.

The courage it takes to face your Trolls

Across thousands of coaching sessions, I've learnt that leaders feel most vulnerable when they share the things their Trolls say to them. It takes enormous courage to speak those words aloud – the cruel accusations and relentless judgements we usually keep hidden.

I've met a lot of Trolls over the years. In truth, I've met far more Trolls than clients. Here's what I know for certain: some of the most capable, impressive people I've worked with carry inner Trolls that say the most breathtakingly harsh things.

These are accusations they would never dream of saying to anyone else. And yet, directed at themselves, they feel entirely plausible. Often, the shame these Trolls provoke is so deep that clients believe they must keep these thoughts secret, sometimes for decades.

Troll facts

Here's what I've learnt about Trolls:

Everyone has them

It may comfort or horrify you to know this, but everyone has Trolls – even the people who seem outrageously confident and self-assured.

Some voice their Troll-talk out loud ("You spoke well in that meeting." "Oh no, I was dreadful – I made no sense and caved too quickly."). Others hide it completely, maintaining a polished surface while waging silent wars inside.

Trolls are human, ancient and universal

Trolls are part of our wiring. Their messages stem from the same instincts that once kept humans safe and accepted within the group. Being excluded from the group used to mean real danger, so the Trolls evolved as an internal early-warning system: "Be careful. Don't draw attention. Don't risk being rejected."

Trolls grow from experience

Their voices often embed so deeply and over so many years that they feel hard-wired to our identity. We gather them along the way – from childhood, adolescence, workplaces, relationships and societal expectations. Some Trolls we can trace directly to a person or moment; others simply arrive and settle in quietly, shaping us without our noticing.

Case study: Stoic Simon

Simon grew up in a family where creating extra work for anyone else was frowned upon. Stoicism wasn't specifically praised, but any request for help was criticized.

As an adult, Simon's Troll berated him every time he caused "inconvenience" to someone. It told him his needs should always come second, that he should tolerate discomfort rather than ask for support.

As a result: he took on an enormous workload without complaint and developed a deeply ingrained habit of overworking – mopping up tasks that could and should have been handled by others. Following his Troll's rules diminished his leadership influence, eroded his wellbeing and slowly sapped his effectiveness.

Case study: Second-rate Wayne

Wayne was MD of a trade association when his CEO resigned unexpectedly. With little time to plan, the board asked Wayne to hold the fort while they recruited a replacement. Six months later, the search had failed – and the board asked Wayne to take on the CEO role permanently.

He accepted, gladly. But a new Troll appeared almost instantly: "You weren't their first choice. No one believes you're good enough. They only gave you the job because they were desperate."

I met Wayne four years into his highly successful tenure, but this Troll still ambushed him daily. No matter how many results he delivered, its narrative stayed the same: "You are not good enough."

Where Trolls come from

Some Trolls grow from personal experience. Others are shaped by the culture, society and times we live in.

Take the body-shaming Troll: perhaps the most universal of them all. Fed by relentless streams of curated images, it whispers that you're too fat, too thin, too short, too tall, too *something*. This Troll has been bred by centuries of conditioning and amplified by modern media – a perfect example of how our environments invite shame into our inner worlds.

Trolls can also surge in response to certain triggers: moments of change, competition or exposure. They thrive when we feel vulnerable – and they love to show up just when we think we've got our act together.

Case study: Invisible Sally

In my early years as a coach, I kept crossing paths with a fellow coach I'd met on a training course (let's call her Vanessa). Her approach to building her business couldn't have been more different from mine.

I was quietly and steadily growing my client base, trusting that good work would lead to recommendations. Vanessa's style was the opposite: bold, outspoken, relentlessly visible. She promoted herself wherever she could – and it worked. Within months, she was being featured in the national press.

For me, that kind of self-promotion would have felt utterly incongruent. And yet, a Troll was born:

> "You should be more like Vanessa. You're invisible, too low-profile, too timid. She's so much better at promoting herself than you – you are rubbish at it. You're going to fail – and she's going to get *all* the clients."

Trolls, like Alarmists, love to catastrophize when given the chance.

The truth was, Vanessa and I weren't in competition. We were destined to attract entirely different kinds of clients – and there were more than enough to go around. But Trolls don't care about facts or nuance.

The land of scarcity

Trolls come from the *land of scarcity*. They operate from a worldview that insists there's a limited supply of success, money, opportunity and belonging. They drive you relentlessly to win the prize – while simultaneously whispering that you're unworthy of it.

This "pincer movement" is their masterstroke: keeping you frozen between the fear of trying and the fear of failing.

A hallmark of Troll-speak is its *absolutism*. Trolls refuse to acknowledge nuance, progress or personal growth. They dismiss your talents, belittle your achievements and insist that whatever you do it'll never be enough. They thrive on comparison, measuring you against others in ways that always leave you lacking.

The Troll's voice is one of shame, blame, belittlement and contempt. While they narrate your life from this harsh perspective, you're out there trying to lead, make decisions, inspire others and show up with confidence.

Living under the Troll narrative

For some of people, the Troll commentary is relentless – a near-constant background hum. Over time, they become so used to this critical inner dialogue that they adjust their behaviour in response, often unconsciously.

For others, the experience is more situational – triggered by moments of transition, exposure or stretch. Any form of change can awaken the Trolls: starting a new job, beginning a relationship, launching a project, even joining a new gym. Whenever you step outside your comfort zone, the Trolls appear.

My own Troll chorus

Deciding to write this book gave my Trolls a field day. Twenty-five years of professional confidence dissolved the moment I became a beginner again – and not just any beginner, but an *ignorant* one.

I knew nothing about publishing. (Honestly, my vision of being a writer was based entirely on Carrie Bradshaw – occasionally tapping away at her New York window, looking glamorous. That was about the extent of my research.)

The more I learned, the more the Trolls swarmed:

> "You should be writing faster. You're too slow. Everyone's bored of waiting. You're ridiculous."
>
> "Just because you can coach people, it doesn't mean you can write something that matters. You're overreaching. You'll be exposed as a fraud."
>
> "Real writers get up at dawn and glide into flow. You procrastinate with laundry and bookshelf arranging. You're lazy and undisciplined."
>
> "If this were meant to happen, it would come easily. But it's not – and soon the world will know your failure."

And then came the kicker:

> "Don't write any of this down in your stupid book. It's too embarrassing. These are your secret shames. If you share them, everyone will have proof of your inadequacy."

Sound familiar? Like internet Trolls hiding behind screens, our inner Trolls thrive on anonymity – firing off cruel, undermining messages from the shadows.

Case study: Pritti, Frankie and Philippe – facing their Trolls

We first met Pritti, Frankie and Philippe in Chapters 7 and 8, each caught in patterns shaped by fear:

- Pritti, recently promoted, avoided challenging her more senior colleagues.
- Frankie clung tightly to control, afraid of showing any vulnerability.
- Philippe stayed in the shadows, reluctant to step into visible leadership.

Now, let's revisit them through the lens of their Trolls – and see what happened when they chose courage instead.

Pritti: Finding her equal place at the table

Pritti's Troll was loud and persistent:

> "You're too young and inexperienced. You've fooled them into thinking you can do this job. You'll soon be found out. They'll never take you seriously."

That inner narrative kept her playing safe. She avoided confrontation, holding back from challenging the opinions and decisions of her older, more experienced colleagues. Instead, she relied on her natural charm, going on a "winning people over" campaign. But the more she tried to please, the less gravitas she carried – and her influence dwindled.

Through coaching, Pritti learned to recognize this voice as a Troll. By externalizing it, she created the space to respond differently.

She started working intentionally on her presence in meetings, combining her natural warmth and energy with a quieter, grounded confidence. She began approaching senior colleagues as equals, leaning into their experience rather than hiding from it. By asking smart questions, listening carefully and showing respect for their expertise, she earned their trust – and found they were ready to hear her views too.

Pritti stopped seeing her youth as a weakness. By taming her Troll and balancing enthusiasm with calm authority, she discovered she could engage fully, even in the trickiest conversations.

Frankie: Leading with vulnerability

Frankie's Troll had a different tactic – equating vulnerability with weak leadership:

> "Your team only respects you because they think you're invincible. If they realize you don't have all the answers, they'll lose faith in you – and in this business. You have to stay strong. Don't let them see you struggle."

For years, Frankie listened. She carried every decision, micromanaged every detail and quietly battled exhaustion. But the pressure was suffocating her – and stifling her team's growth too.

Through coaching, Frankie saw the pattern clearly: protecting herself from appearing vulnerable was limiting everyone's potential. So, she took a bold step.

At an all-company meeting, she spoke candidly about her leadership style:

> "I've realized I've been holding too much, trying to be across everything. I trust you. I value your expertise. And I want to lead differently – to create space for all of us to bring our best."

The warmth of the response took her by surprise. Her team had seen her struggling but didn't know how to help. By expressing her vulnerability and asking for their partnership, she gained more respect, not less.

From there, everything shifted. Frankie began delegating meaningfully, encouraging her team to step up, and focusing her energy where she could have the most impact. By quieting her Troll, she unlocked her people's untapped potential – and her own.

Philippe: From likeable to leaderlike

Philippe's Troll whispered a more insidious message:

> "You only got the CEO job because everyone likes you, not because you can lead. You're not decisive enough, not tough enough – and when the board realizes that, you'll be out. Keep your head down, don't upset anyone, and maybe you'll get away with it."

For months, Philippe followed that voice. He avoided confrontation, stayed quiet in board meetings and prioritized being liked over being respected. But slowly, he realized his desire to stay safe was undermining the business and the people who relied on him.

Through coaching, Philippe came to see that true care for his team meant being willing to do hard things – even when this risked disapproval.

He began practising small, courageous acts: speaking up in board meetings, pushing back where needed and making decisions guided by what was best for the company, not what would keep everyone happy.

The turning point came when he advocated fiercely for his people during a high-stakes negotiation with the investors. By standing up to the board – calmly, clearly and with conviction – he earned their respect. More importantly, he earned his own.

Philippe discovered that courage didn't require abandoning his collaborative, compassionate style. It meant integrating it with strength and clarity – and trusting that respect would follow authenticity.

The bigger picture

Pritti, Frankie and Philippe faced very different challenges, yet their Trolls had one thing in common: they worked to keep them safe but small.

- Pritti's Troll tried to convince her she was too inexperienced.
- Frankie's Troll told her she had to be invincible.
- Philippe's Troll insisted that being liked mattered more than being effective.

Each of them discovered that by externalizing those voices, they lost their grip. Each leader claimed their Graceful Power, stepping into new levels of influence.

You can do the same.

A note on imposter syndrome

Imposter syndrome is the Troll narrative with the best PR machine behind it. Thanks to media coverage, most of us are now familiar with this internal monologue. I seem to hear women talk about imposter syndrome more often than men, but in coaching leaders I see no gender bias at all. Perhaps the difference is that more women are more willing to express their self-doubt openly, whereas more men tend to manage the experience privately.

The Troll's message, though, is always the same:

> "You're not good enough for this job. You don't have the skills, the intelligence, the experience or the aptitude to succeed. You've been lucky so far, but any day now you'll be found out. Then, you'll be exposed and humiliated. Best to keep your head down, play it safe and hope you get away with it."

That looming fear of being found out – of being exposed as the talentless imposter you Troll believes you to be – triggers a full-blown fear response: Your heart races, your breath shortens, your throat tightens, your stomach drops and in that heightened state, your Troll pushes you toward one of three reactions:

- **Fight:** You charge in with unnecessary intensity – overly assertive, even aggressive.
- **Flight:** You play it safe, staying quiet, preserving the status quo, pleasing or placating others to avoid attention.
- **Freeze:** You sidestep opportunities for stretch, convincing yourself they're not worth the effort or the risk.

Left unrecognized, this can quietly shape careers, relationships and leadership impact for years.

Bad news and good news

The *bad* news: you will never be entirely free of your Trolls. They are a feature of being human, hardwired into your survival system. Each time you edge toward growth – or dare to step beyond your comfort zone – they'll appear, right on cue. Their messages are familiar: "You're not up to this"; "You're bound to fail"; "Save yourself. Play safe. Back away."

The *good* news: dancing to their tune is optional. You *can* learn to tame your Trolls – and with practice, you can reduce their power to the point that you barely even notice them.

When you free yourself from the tyranny of your Trolls, recognizing their voices for what they are, you create the space to hear something else: your *wise inner voice* – the one that brings perspective, discernment and possibility. That's the voice that lets you act with courage rather than react from fear.

Every time you choose courage over compliance, you grow your capacity to lead with Graceful Power.

"I fear my Trolls are the secret to my success!"

Several clients have confessed to me that they're afraid of letting go of their Trolls, worried these voices might be the source of their motivation. "Without them," they ask, "would I even get out of bed in the morning?"

If this feels familiar, let's explore it.

It's true that the constant criticism of our Trolls can trigger a physiological fear response: adrenaline surges, glucose floods the bloodstream and your body prepares for action. It can feel energizing – even productive. You get up, get moving, push harder. You take on the challenge, work the extra hours, fend off the competition and avoid being "found out" as the fraud your Troll insists you are.

It works. Many highly successful people have fuelled themselves this way. But at what cost?

This defensive, fear-driven approach keeps you locked in the *defensive zone* of the spectrum of all possible outcomes. As with the warnings of the Alarmists, your Troll talk may contain some useful information. But when those truths are wrapped in derision, blame and contempt, it becomes almost impossible to separate what's helpful from what's harmful.

When your inner world is dominated by constant criticism and judgement, you start to believe everyone else sees you the same way. Eventually, you show up in the world as though that story is true: defensive, reactive and closed off. Rather than leading from possibility, you're fearfully striving to avoid exposure.

We can become so used to being guided by these inner voices that we lose connection with something far more valuable: our wise inner voice. The one that brings clarity, choice and courage – the courage to lead with Graceful Power.

In the next chapter, we'll explore how to reconnect with that inner voice. But first, there's one more essential step: you need to get to know your Trolls more intimately. To tame them, you need to know them.

Getting to know your Trolls

By now, you've probably recognized some of your own Troll-talk. Some voices are obvious – loud, direct and relentless. Others are more cunning, slipping into your thoughts so subtly that you act on their advice without even realizing it.

So how do you spot them?

The first clues are often *physical*. Trolls trigger the body's fear response. I often notice that my clients literally shrink when they are sitting with their Troll – sitting low in their chair, a little hunched, less animated – they literally take up less space. Whilst writing about Trolls, I've been aware of my own feelings of fear. As I type, I notice mild nausea, shallower breaths and a restlessness in my core. Alongside that comes a strong urge to escape: check my phone, respond to emails, tidy my desk – anything other than stay with the discomfort. My Trolls whisper: "Stop. Do something easier. You don't want to write this."

These sensations in your body are valuable signals. If you pause and pay attention, you'll notice what often comes next: the thoughts and stories your Trolls weave.

They seed doubts about your worth, question your capability and feed your fears of inadequacy, failure or rejection. They can sound rational – even helpful – but the impact is always limiting. Trolls thrive on guilt, shame, anxiety and disappointment. Like the Alarmists, they're trying to keep you safe. But in doing so, they keep you small.

When we listen to these voices, they spark an urgent need to act, pushing you to resolve the discomfort as quickly as possible. Typically, that action takes one of three forms: Avoiding, averting or attacking.

Avoiding

Avoiding is the most passive strategy. It means staying away from the situation altogether – stepping back rather than stepping in. You convince yourself it's better not to act, but then nothing actually changes.

Avoiding can look like:

- Procrastinating on the task that matters most.
- Ruminating endlessly instead of deciding.
- Quietly deprioritizing what feels uncomfortable.
- Handing work off unnecessarily.
- Filling your time with busy work that feels productive but achieves less.

Avoidance provides temporary relief but costs you influence, energy and opportunities for growth.

Averting

Averting is more active. Instead of ignoring the situation, you work around it – taking pre-emptive action to sidestep potential discomfort or conflict altogether. On the surface, it looks strategic, but it comes from fear rather than choice.

Averting can look like:

- People-pleasing to smooth over tension.
- Switching roles or projects to escape potential failure.
- Strategically withdrawing from situations where you might be exposed.
- Placating others to avoid disagreement.
- Choosing a "safer" path that limits your growth.

Averting protects your sense of safety in the short term but keeps you from testing your full capability.

Attacking

Attacking is the opposite response: confronting the situation head-on. Fuelled by the surge of adrenaline your Trolls provoke, you go in hard, often unconsciously using force or control to manage the discomfort.

Attacking can look like:

- Being overly directive and controlling.
- Arguing aggressively or defensively.
- Using sharp, critical language.
- Pushing through conversations or decisions just to end the tension.

It can feel decisive in the moment, but because the action comes from fear, it rarely delivers your best leadership.

Only by becoming acutely aware of when Troll-talk is present – and how it affects you physically, emotionally and mentally – can you create the space for conscious choice. The choice between reacting from fear and responding with courage – leading with Graceful Power.

Exercise: Recognizing and taming your Trolls

The goal here is not to silence or deny these voices, but to recognize them so clearly that you can turn your attention towards a wiser, more measured source of guidance. That means practising something most of us would rather avoid: sitting with the discomfort they create.

Step 1: Meet your Troll

Choose one of your strongest Trolls – the one whose voice shows up most often. Imagine placing it somewhere in the room in front of you.

- What does it look like?
- How does it move?
- What's the tone of its voice?
- Most importantly: *what does it say to you?*

Be honest here. Grab your notebook and write down everything that comes to mind. Don't edit yourself. Don't make it polite. Let the voice speak exactly as it does in your head – even if it gets louder, meaner or more extreme.

Tip: Think of the *catastrophe zone* from the spectrum of all possible outcomes – this is the equivalent for your Troll's narrative. Push it right to the edges. As you do this, keep reminding yourself: *This is not you. These are not facts.*

This is the judgement of an imaginary voice – one you've been reacting to, but don't have to obey.

Step 2: Spot the traits of Troll-talk

Trolls are cunning but predictable. They use familiar tactics to hook your attention. Here's what to listen for.

Absolute language

Trolls speak in extremes:

- Not "You were a bit slow writing that report," but "You are lazy."
- Not "It might have been better to listen first," but "You never listen."

Negative comparisons

Trolls love measuring you against others – but only when it leaves you feeling "less than":

- "If only you were as diligent as Aadi."
- "Everyone wants specialists now – you're irrelevant."

Guilt triggers

They're fluent in guilt-inducing phrases disguised as "helpful feedback":

- "You should be more dynamic."

- "Why can't you focus on one thing at a time?"
- "You could be a good leader... if only you had a backbone."

Never satisfied

No matter what you achieve, your Troll won't be impressed. It will quietly move the goalposts every time.

Fights dirty

When your Troll senses you're ignoring it, it panics. It turns up the volume or attacks the process itself:

- "This exercise is stupid."
- "Without me, you'll be found out."
- "I'm the only reason you've succeeded so far."

If you notice that kind of pushback, smile – it means you're starting to gain the upper hand.

Step 3: Notice the things you'd never say

Once you've captured your Troll's words, pause and read them back. Now imagine saying those same lines to someone you care about – a friend, partner, child or colleague. You wouldn't, would you?

The things we allow our Trolls to say to us are often things we would never say to anyone else. You don't deserve to be spoken to that way, even by an imaginary voice.

Step 4: Stop feeding the Troll

Trolls have only one source of energy: **your attention**. The more you engage with them, the stronger they become. Once you've recognized their voice, notice the subtle ways you might unintentionally be fuelling them:

- **Listening to them:** Replaying their accusations, scanning for proof, debating the accuracy of their judgements.
- **Believing them:** Accepting their verdict as fact and shrinking under its weight.
- **Sharing their views:** Repeating their thoughts out loud. Undermining yourself before anyone else can. Putting yourself down, even as a joke.
- **Defending yourself:** Arguing back in your head. Trying to reason with a voice that doesn't listen.
- **Presenting evidence:** Scrambling to prove your worthiness with past successes or credentials.
- **Behaving reactively:** Obeying their warnings or overcompensating to prove them wrong.

The moment you spot yourself doing one of these, pause. Every time you withdraw your attention, you weaken their influence.

Step 5: Taming your Trolls

Taming your Trolls takes practice – but you already have more power than you think.

Insist on separation

Hear Troll-talk for what it really is: a dialogue between *you* and an *imaginary voice*. You are under no obligation to participate. When you hear it, name it clearly: "Ah, there you are – I recognize you. You're a Troll."

Sharpen anticipation

Pay attention to the triggers that bring your Trolls to life: specific situations, environments, types of people or moments of change. New roles, public speaking, pitching ideas – these are classic flare-ups. As the saying goes: "forewarned is forearmed." The better you can anticipate them, the better prepared you'll be.

Identify and disengage

When your Troll shows up, catch it quickly and name it. Then break the spell by disrupting the mind–body connection of the fear response loop we explored earlier in this chapter. Move your body:

- If you're in a meeting, step out briefly, walk across the room or fetch a glass of water.
- If you're alone, stretch, open a window or take a break and change location.
- As you move, take your Troll with you and imagine leaving it somewhere far away – dropped out of the window or locked in a drawer – reinforcing that sense of separation.

One leader I coached used a clever tactic when speaking to large groups. He deliberately placed his water glass on the far side of the podium. When his Troll appeared, he'd calmly walk over, take a sip and – in his mind – place the Troll under the table before returning to centre stage. The routine was so intentional that, over time, he rarely needed it at all.

Take charge

You may not be able to stop your Trolls from showing up, but you can choose how you respond:

- You are not required to listen.
- You are not required to engage.
- You are free to refocus on what matters.

Your Trolls won't disappear completely – and that's okay. What matters is recognizing them for what they are. The moment you pause and notice – "Ah, there's my Troll again" – you create space for choice. You don't need to fight them, obey them or silence them. You simply need to see them clearly and decide where you want to place your attention.

UNLOCKING YOUR COURAGE

You've now learned how to manage your Alarmists and Trolls – those two noisy inner tribes that stir up anxiety and self-doubt. You've calmed the fear-driven voices warning of catastrophe, and you've learned to separate your sense of self from the relentless inner critic.

However, sometimes, taming your Trolls and calming your Alarmists isn't quite enough. You've quieted the noise, but the silence that follows doesn't always fill itself with courage or clarity. You might still feel restless, uncertain or unsure what action to take.

That's where the next set of techniques comes in. These tools are designed to help you access your steady, courageous centre beneath the noise – the wise inner voice that's waiting beneath the doubt and distraction. These techniques will help you reconnect with your values, find clarity in uncertainty, and take action from a place of strength, intention and Graceful Power.

Technique: Consult your Wise Tribe

Once your inner Alarmists and Trolls are tamed, you have the chance to bring in a different tribe – one that uplifts, inspires and guides you when the stakes feel high.

Your *Wise Tribe* is made up of role models, mentors and guidance-givers – people who embody qualities you admire and who, in your imagination, can help you see your situation more clearly.

How to build your Wise Tribe:

- Choose three to six people whose qualities and approach to life inspire you.

- They might be personal mentors, public figures, fictional characters or even your Future Self from Chapter 5.
- You don't need to know them personally; you only need to know or sense enough about them to imagine how they might guide you.

For each member of this Wise Tribe, use the template over the page (or download a copy via the QR code in the Introduction) to capture:

- The characteristics, passions and beliefs you admire.
- The advice you imagine they'd give you.
- The qualities that unite you.
- The rallying cry you'd stand behind together.

I've built my own Wise Tribe over the years. Among others, it includes Lady Gaga, Glen Mills (sprinting coach to Usain Bolt) and Sarah Connor from *The Terminator*. I don't know any of them personally, nor do I know a great deal about them – but I perceive qualities in them that inspire me: creative courage, relentless belief and fierce resilience.

Whenever my Trolls tell me, "You can't coach this leader – you're out of your depth", I picture Glen Mills. I imagine him reminding me that my role isn't to be a better leader than my clients – it's to be the best coach I can be. That's my lane. That's my power.

You might choose to create a visual representation of your Wise Tribe – gathering images to be kept somewhere visible.

Then, when you're feeling stuck or uncertain, consult your tribe. Ask: "What would they do in my position?" It can be remarkably clarifying.

	Tribe member 1	Tribe member 2	Tribe member 3
Name:			
Expertise:			
Most admirable characteristics:			
Personal passion:			
Guiding belief:			
Advice they give:			
What unites us?			
Rallying cry:			

Technique: Grounding in time and space visualization

Sometimes courage emerges most easily when we pause, quiet our mind and allow our inner wisdom to emerge.

Follow the QR code in the Introduction to access a guided visualization designed to bring you into the present moment and help you find clarity when your thoughts are spinning.

Find a quiet space where you won't be interrupted, close your eyes and let yourself be guided through the process. Even if you don't think of yourself as "good at these things", you may be surprised by the experience.

With practice, you'll be able to access this calm, steady place even without the recording – anytime you need grounding and perspective.

Technique: The want/need check

When the fearful voices are whispering, everything feels tangled and the way forward is unclear, two simple questions can bring you back to centre:

1. What do I *want* to do?
2. What do I *need* to do?

Sometimes, the answers align beautifully and the path forward becomes obvious. But often, especially in leadership, they don't. Those moments call for courage – to acknowledge the discomfort and act on what matters most.

For example:
You've noticed an influential colleague undermining one of your team members in meetings. It's happening repeatedly and your Troll is whispering: "Stay out of it. Keep the peace. Don't rock the boat."

- **What you want to do:** Look away. Hope the behaviour stops. Avoid the confrontation.
- **What you need to do:** Give feedback to the colleague. Protect your team member's confidence. Preserve trust within the group.

When want and need diverge, that tension is your *invitation to courage*.

Technique: Abundant reframing

Trolls love a *scarcity mindset* – the belief that there's not enough to go around. Not enough resources, credit, success or opportunity. It's a primal fear, rooted in survival instincts, amplified by the pressures of modern life.

But in leadership, scarcity thinking shrinks your impact. It drives competition instead of collaboration. It makes you hoard visibility, defend credit and protect influence, instead of sharing and multiplying it.

The alternative is *abundant thinking* – the belief that success isn't finite, and that by lifting others, you also lift yourself. The table below gives some examples.

Scarcity thought	Abundant reframe	Practice
"There can be only one winner."	"There's room for many kinds of success."	Notice comparison creeping in and return to your own definition of success.
"If they get promoted, I never will."	"New opportunities are created all the time."	Celebrate a colleague's success out loud – let generosity build trust.
"I must fight for recognition."	"Recognition grows when I share it."	Acknowledge one person each week who's contributed to your success.
"New hires threaten my position."	"They bring energy and ideas that make us all better."	Invite collaboration or mentoring moments; create two-way learning.
"I can't delegate or rest – I'll fall behind."	"Rest and collaboration fuel sustainable leadership."	Block short recovery windows; choose one task to delegate fully this week.
"We must hoard our expertise."	"Sharing knowledge strengthens all our outcomes."	Share one insight or practice from your team with peers or partners.

Abundance thinking doesn't deny challenge. It simply refuses to be controlled by the fear of "not enough". It trusts that energy, ideas and influence can be replenished – and that generosity can be contagious too.

A leader grounded in abundance lifts others without losing ground themselves. That is Graceful Power in action.

Technique: The Kind Mind audit

The *Kind Mind* is your antidote to Troll-talk. It's a voice of honesty and care – a calm, fair-minded observer who sees things as they are, without distortion or judgement.

The goal isn't flattery or sugar-coating. A Kind Mind reflects reality clearly:

- It acknowledges what's working.
- It recognizes where you're holding back.
- It invites you to stretch with courage – without shame or criticism.

Find a quiet moment at the end of your day. Reflect gently on these prompts:

- What did I handle well today?
- Which strengths or qualities did I draw on?
- Where did I hold back or hesitate?
- What might I try differently next time?
- What would my Kind Mind say to me right now?

This isn't about overanalysing. Stay close to what actually happened. Let insight, not judgement, be your guide.

You can also use a Kind Mind Audit *before* a challenging moment – a meeting, a presentation or a high-stakes conversation. Taking a few minutes to reconnect with your strengths and values can steady you, calm the noise and set you up to act with courage.

Courage doesn't need to be a roar. Often, it's quiet – a steady voice beneath the noise of your Alarmists and Trolls.

The techniques in this chapter are tools to help you access that steadier place when fear or uncertainty cloud your judgement. They're not about silencing the discomfort, but about learning to move with it and through it.

With practice, these daily acts of courage compound into something bigger: a stronger, calmer, more grounded connection to your own Graceful Power.

PART IV

COMPASSION

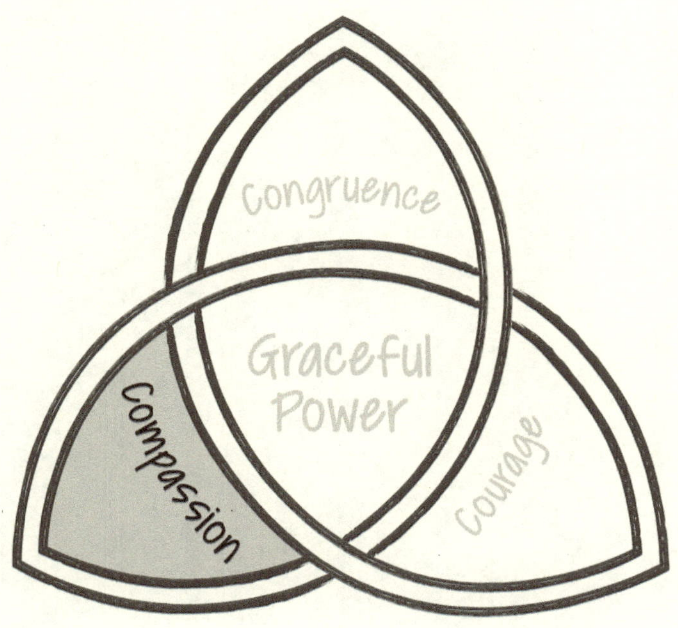

In this part of the book, we'll explore how compassion strengthens your Graceful Power and enables you to build thriving relationships, unlock potential and create environments where people bring their best:

- Chapter 10 – *The role of compassion in Graceful Power.* We'll explore the role of compassion in modern leadership – including the often-overlooked practice of *self-compassion* – and the hallmarks of truly compassionate leaders who combine strength, clarity and care.
- Chapter 11 – *A mindset and a skillset.* Here, we'll develop the practical foundations of compassionate leadership: *deep listening, leading with curiosity* and *believing in potential.* These practices expand your ability to connect meaningfully, unlock trust and inspire growth in others.
- Chapter 12 – *Creating a climate of flourishing.* Finally, we'll look at how compassionate leaders intentionally shape the cultural and emotional conditions where motivation, wellbeing and performance thrive – helping individuals, teams and organizations flourish.

By the end of this section, you'll understand how compassion enables you to lead with *humanity* and *high impact* – seeing people clearly, supporting them fully and creating the conditions for them to succeed. When combined with congruence and courage, compassion completes the foundation of Graceful Power – enabling you to meet complexity with clarity, lead with influence rather than force and leave a lasting, positive mark on the people and systems you touch.

Chapter 10

The role of compassion in Graceful Power

Over the past 25 years coaching senior leaders across different sectors – from high-growth startups to established global organizations – I've come to see compassion not as a "soft skill" but as a core leadership capability. It's one of the core attributes that enables leaders to meet the complex and sometimes conflicting demands of modern leadership: delivering results while developing people.

Compassionate leadership captures a paradox at the heart of effective leadership today: the need to be both an empathetic guide and a performance-driven manager. Leaders are being asked to care deeply about their teams' wellbeing *and* to hold them accountable for results. Compassion isn't just about being nice – it's about being effective.

In fact, research shows that compassionate leadership results in better outcomes across the board. A 2023 study from *Harvard Business Review*[1] found that leaders who demonstrate compassion foster higher trust, collaboration and job satisfaction – all of which directly correlate with improved performance.

Navigating the tension between showing that you care *and* that you have high expectations is challenging, especially if your own boss doesn't show much compassion when your targets are missed! It takes energy and commitment to slow down, listen with care and offer support – particularly when someone is underperforming. But leaders with Graceful Power know this investment pays off in the long run, both in performance and in people. The proven benefits of compassionate leadership include:

- Greater trust and loyalty among team members.
- Higher employee engagement and motivation.
- Improved creativity, resilience and collaboration.
- Stronger individual and team performance over time.

Interestingly, research shows the impact of compassionate leadership goes beyond the person who directly receives it – it also shapes how observers see the leader and their work culture. Dutton et al. (2014)[2] found that witnessing compassionate actions at work cultivates shared pride and can inspire others to act for the greater good. Compassion doesn't just inspire the one person it is directed towards – the impact is infectious.

If you've ever had a leader really listen, understand your perspective and adapt a situation to help you succeed, you'll know it makes a difference. You remember them – and you're more willing to go the extra mile for them when it matters.

Yet, despite all the evidence, we still find ourselves in a time when many employees feel they don't truly matter – to their organization, to their boss or even to their colleagues. There is a yearning to feel significant – not just as part of a team, but as individuals with unique value.

As Zach Mercurio, author of *The Power of Mattering at Work*, explains in his HBR[3] article:

> "When people know that they matter at work, they thrive. Mattering enhances self-esteem ('I'm worthy') and self-efficacy ('I'm capable') and strengthens motivation, well-being and performance… Employees who believe they matter report greater satisfaction, are more likely to be promoted, and are less likely to leave."

Compassionate leadership is not just about recognizing struggle. It's about being curious and responsive when people are thriving – noticing the conditions that enable high motivation and fulfilment, and intentionally creating more of them. A compassionate leader wants to understand what drives each team member – and also to deepen their own self-awareness, so the individual, the team and the organization can all take responsibility for creating the conditions for everyone to thrive.

So how do leaders do this?

Through a blend of clear intent, skilful listening, purposeful curiosity and a belief in the greater potential of others – followed by thoughtful action. These are the characteristics of compassion we'll explore in the coming pages.

But first, we need to examine an essential foundation of sustainable leadership: compassion for oneself.

Case study: Compassion starts with you

Savannah and her business partner had spent nearly 20 years building a consultancy from a tiny office into a thriving, respected practice. When they were finally acquired by a major firm, Savannah felt proud – and completely exhausted.

As part of the buyout terms, she had agreed to stay on for another three years. But now, facing the challenge of merging two cultures, new expectations and an unrelenting pace, she found her motivation and energy dwindling.

In our coaching sessions, a pattern became clear: Savannah's deep commitment to her team's wellbeing had come at the expense of her own. Determined to protect her employees' work–life balance, she regularly worked late to improve their reports or presentations, covered gaps in their output and shouldered responsibilities others had let slip.

Savannah had exceptional stamina – but she was stuck in the mindset of a 20-something founder. Now in her early 40s, she was still carrying the weight of the business herself.

The consequences of this imbalance were becoming undeniable:

- Her health and happiness were suffering – she felt increasingly resentful towards her team and engaged with them less and less.

- Her wealth of experience wasn't being deployed to develop the team – she was improving their work *for* them, rather than coaching them to grow.
- Her leadership lacked integrity: she urged her team to look after themselves, while visibly neglecting her own needs.
- Her team had stopped stretching themselves – they knew she would step in if they didn't quite deliver.
- She was making leadership look deeply unappealing – she wasn't thriving and it showed.

Savannah's compassion was real and admirable. But without self-compassion, it had become unsustainable – and ultimately counterproductive. The resentment that crept in when her team left work on time while she stayed late was a signal: something needed to change.

Compassionate leadership must include the leader themself.

Self-compassion

Paying attention to your own needs isn't an indulgence – it's an essential act of responsible leadership. If you're going to lead others with compassion, you need to begin with yourself.

That means tending to your physical, mental and emotional well-being. It also means feeling connected to your purpose and genuinely fulfilled by your work. Only when you're well-resourced – to the best of your ability – can you offer your full and generous attention to those you lead.

The aeroplane oxygen mask analogy captures it perfectly: Put on your own oxygen mask first, before you help anyone else with there's. If you lose consciousness, you are no help to anyone! Likewise, if you're burnt out, chronically stressed or quietly demoralized, how can you wholeheartedly support others to avoid the same fate? Don't think your own state won't go unnoticed, either. The behaviour you model sets the tone, even if unconsciously, for your team or organization.

A 2022 study published in the *Journal of Applied Psychology*[4] demonstrated that leaders who do not engage in self-compassion are less likely to help their team members with both work and personal challenges. The research found that when leaders practiced self-compassion, they were perceived as more competent and engaged – and their teams reported more positive experiences. Conversely, a lack of self-compassion led to less effective leadership behaviours and poorer perceptions of their abilities.

I learnt this lesson early in my career. I worked with a brilliant, high-flying leader who managed a vast portfolio across Europe, the Middle East and Africa. On her good days, she was thoughtful, sharp and kind. But the relentless travel, long hours and heavy responsibility took their toll. Most of the time, she was short-tempered, impatient and hard to please. I didn't feel respected or inspired by her – I felt wary of her.

What stayed with me wasn't just her mood, but the message her behaviour sent: this is what success looks like. Exhaustion, irritation and a complete absence of joy. At the time, I promised myself I'd never take on that kind of international role. A few years later, when exactly the same role became the only obvious next step for me, I left the company rather than accept it.

Of course, I now know it's entirely possible to hold a high-responsibility role and protect your wellbeing. I've worked with leaders whose boundaries are rock-solid, who travel widely and yet stay calm, present and grounded. But that early encounter etched a powerful warning in my memory: without self-compassion, even the most talented leaders lose their impact.

I recently coached a global sales director who travelled extensively and led a large, remote team. What struck me wasn't just her results, but the way she protected her energy. She blocked out Friday afternoons for reflection and family. She declined early morning meetings across time zones and prioritized eight hours sleep over everything. She encouraged her team to build similar boundaries – and backed it up by respecting them.

Her team described her as clear-headed, generous and deeply trustworthy. What they valued most was her presence – the calm, grounded focus that came from her decision to treat herself with respect.

The self-other compassion loop

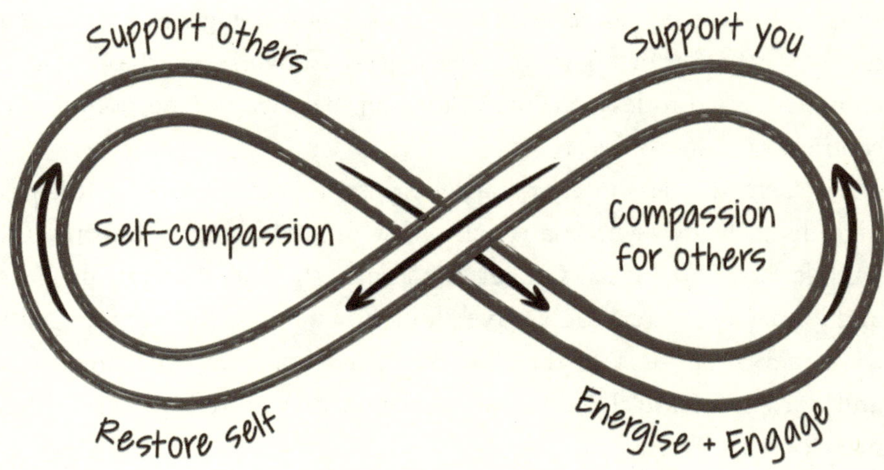

There is reciprocal rhythm between self-compassion and compassion for others. When you restore yourself – through rest, meaning, boundaries or joy – you refill your capacity to support those around you. In turn, as they feel heard, energized and encouraged, they're more likely to perform well, stay engaged and support you when the pressure is on.

Compassionate leadership begins with the leader. Which is why, right now, I'm inviting you to take a pause and reflect on how you're doing – not in the professional, performance-focused sense, but in the whole-life sense.

Exercise: The Wheel of Life

One of the first tools I ever learned as a coach – and one I still return to regularly with clients – is the *Wheel of life*. It helps you step back from the day-to-day to-do list and reflect on the broader terrain of your life.

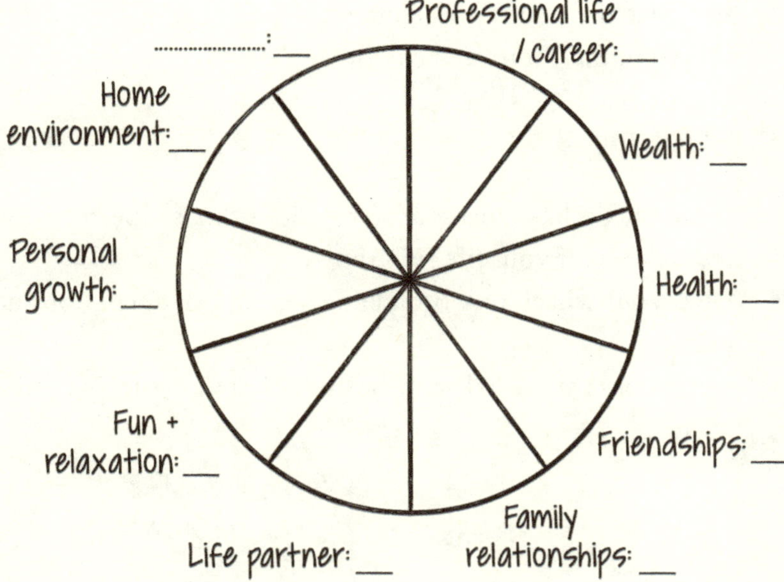

You can simply draw the template into your notebook, or you can download it via the QR code in the Introduction. The wheel is divided into ten segments – nine pre-assigned to key areas of life and one left blank for you to customize. You might use it for something personally important, such as community, spirituality, physical challenge or a side hustle.

Step 1: Assess where you are today

For each area of your life, ask yourself: "How fulfilling is this aspect of my life right now?"

- Give each area a score from 1 (*not at all fulfilled*) to 10 (*totally fulfilled*).
- On the wheel, mark the boundary line for your score in each segment.
- A score of 10 reaches the outer edge of the circle.
- A 9 is just inside it, and so on.

- Connect the marks to create your personal *Wheel of life*. As shown in the completed example.

Pause and reflect:

- What shape has emerged? What does this shape reveal about the balance of your life right now?
- Does your wheel look broad and smooth, or small, lopsided or uneven?
- What does this visual snapshot reveal about your life today?

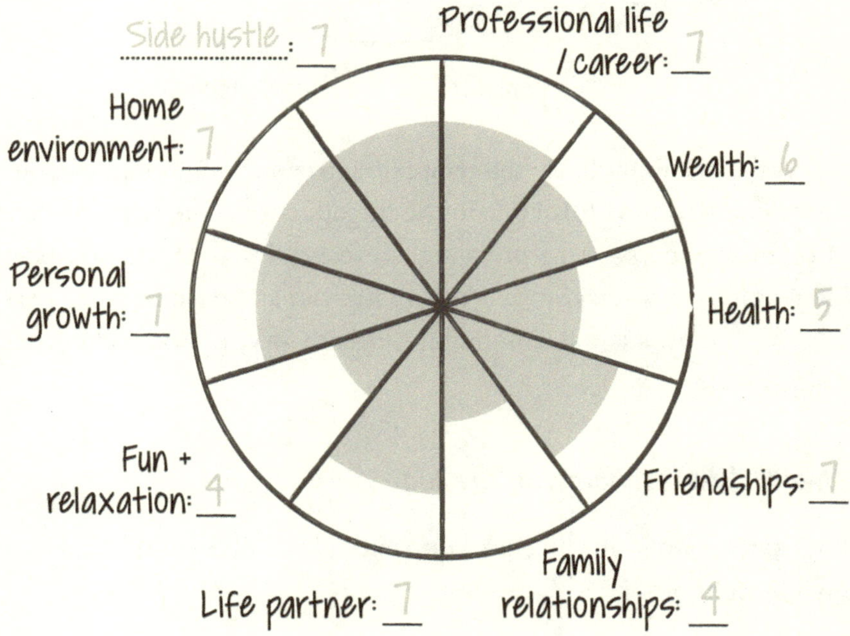

Step 2: Envision your 10/10 life

Before you leap into action, pause to clarify your destination. For each area, write a short statement describing what a *10/10 fulfilled life* would look like.

- Think long-term: what would feel true not just next week, but a year or even ten years from now?
- Focus on how you want to *feel*, rather than ticking off short-term goals.

For example:

- In the area of health, a statement like "My body feels fit and strong" is more powerful than "I go to the gym twice a week and have lost 2kg".
- The first reflects your *overall vision* and desired experience, while the second locks you into a temporary, narrow outcome.

These statements become your *signposts* – helping you stay focused on what really matters as you make choices and set priorities.

Step 3: Choose your first micro-actions

Now that you've imagined your ideal state, identify one or two small, specific actions you can take this week to move closer to that vision.

- Keep the actions simple and achievable – small enough that you cannot fail to take the first step.
- Break larger goals into micro-actions as necessary. Tiny, consistent acts of progress that will add up to significant change.

Step 4: Build in accountability

Commit to revisiting your Wheel of life, fulfillment statements and action plan in a week:

- Schedule a short review session in your calendar.
- Use it to check progress, celebrate small wins and choose your next set of micro-actions.

This exercise is not about achieving instant balance – life rarely works that way. The idea is to become more *conscious* and *intentional* about where your energy goes, and to make steady, manageable shifts towards the life you want to create.

The reflective work you've done earlier in this book will feed into this exercise. Perhaps there's a value you're neglecting in one area of life – or over-expressing in another.

Look to your Future Self for guidance on what you need right now to improve the balance and reward of your life.

You may also need courage here. Self-compassion doesn't always mean saying no to things, sometimes it means saying yes to uncomfortable changes or revealing a vulnerability. Ending a project, initiating a difficult conversation or admitting that something isn't working.

By committing to regular and intentional acts of self-compassion, you will soon experience an expansion in your sense of fulfilment and a renewed willingness to support others in creating their own fuller life experience.

Leaders always shape the workplace climate. Often without knowing it, you influence how people feel, how they behave, what they expect. Think back: where have you recently been a positive influence? And, honestly, where might your stress, distraction or self-neglect have shaped something less helpful?

Try reflecting on this question for a moment. What comes up for you?

> "If I changed just one thing for myself, what would have the greatest positive impact on the wellbeing and productivity of my team?"

Leading with compassion begins with giving yourself permission to prioritize you. Self-compassion is essential for Graceful Power:

- It strengthens *congruence*, by helping you live in alignment with your values rather than running on empty or autopilot.
- It fuels *courage*, by giving you the clarity and energy to make difficult choices that serve your long-term growth.

- It deepens *compassion*, because when you're resourced and centred, you're more able to show up with care and generosity for others.

Without self-compassion, even the most committed leaders can become reactive, resentful or performative. With it, your leadership becomes more authentic, more effective and more graceful.

Hallmarks of compassion in leadership

Up to now, we've explored how prioritizing your own needs fuels your ability to lead with compassion. When you manage your energy, respect your boundaries and care for yourself, you create the inner capacity to extend that same care to others.

Now, let's change our focus to explore the experience of being led by someone who demonstrates compassion for their people.

Reflect on your own experience

Think back over your working life so far and recall two managers who had the biggest impact on you – one positive and one negative:

- The first is the manager who most hindered or frustrated your professional growth at the time – let's call them your Bad Boss.
- The second is the manager with whom your growth accelerated most positively – we'll call this person your Great Boss.

Take a moment to picture them both clearly.

- How did they behave?
- What did they do – or fail to do – that shaped your performance and experience at work?
- How did each make you *feel* about yourself, your abilities and your potential?

Grab your notebook and sketch two simple columns as shown below.

Bad boss - detrimental to my growth	Great boss - accelerated my growth
Typical behaviours	Typical behaviours
•	•
•	•
•	•
•	•
•	•
•	•

Fill them in as fully as you can – list the patterns, the decisions and the actions that made the difference.

Over the years, I've asked many leaders in coaching sessions and workshops to do this exact reflection. The patterns are remarkably consistent.

Your Great Boss – the one who helped you flourish – almost certainly demonstrated many of these *hallmarks of compassionate leadership*:

- **Paid attention to you:** Seeing you as a whole person, not just a performer. They listened carefully and genuinely, with interest in your challenges, frustrations, successes and aspirations.
- **Sought to understand you:** Investing time to explore your perspective and experience, showing curiosity about what you needed to give your best.
- **Showed empathy:** Recognizing and validating your emotions, sometimes even helping you gain insight into your situation and move forward with greater clarity.

- **Demonstrated belief in your potential:** Offering encouragement, stretching assignments and feedback designed to grow your skills and confidence.
- **Held a shared focus:** Consistently linking your work and growth to a bigger purpose, mission or vision.
- **Took thoughtful, intelligent action:** Created the conditions where you and your team could thrive:
  - Removing obstacles, such as conflicts, excessive workloads or unclear priorities.
  - Providing resources, whether people, tools, training or time.
  - Creating a safe and supportive environment where learning, experimentation and growth were encouraged – even through setbacks.

In contrast, your Bad Boss, at least in terms of your professional growth, likely displayed few – if any – of these characteristics.

Can you recall how these two different managers made you feel about yourself and what you were capable of?

It's often the emotional residue that's most revealing. We rarely forget how someone made us feel.

Compassionate leadership begins with you – and it flows outward. When you respect your own boundaries, tend to your energy and connect with what gives you meaning, you create the capacity to listen deeply, support others and lead with clarity and strength. Compassion fuels performance, but it also shapes culture – it sets the tone for how people relate to one another and how they show up for the collective purpose.

The impact is contagious. When leaders act with compassion, they don't just support the individual in front of them – they influence the wider team, the culture and even the way people perceive their organization. When we witness compassion, we feel inspired, proud and more willing to contribute to the greater good. That's the kind of leadership today's world is calling for.

In the next chapter, we'll look at *how* to bring compassion to life in your leadership – the mindset to adopt, the skillset to practise and the everyday actions that turn care into impact. We'll explore how to create the conditions where people feel heard, valued and empowered to thrive – including you.

Chapter 11

A mindset and a skillset

Compassionate leadership begins with intention, but it's brought to life through action. In Chapter 10, we explored why compassion matters – how it fuels performance, builds trust and shapes culture. Now, we turn to the practical side: the mindset and skillset you need to lead compassionately in real, everyday moments.

Compassion shows up in small, deliberate choices – how you listen, what you notice, the questions you ask and how you respond. It's the cumulative effect of hundreds of moments where people feel seen, valued and supported.

In this chapter, we'll explore three essential practices that bring compassionate leadership to life:

1. **Listening:** Giving your full attention so others feel truly heard.
2. **Curiosity:** Seeking to understand before you seek to be understood.
3. **Belief in potential:** Holding a vision of others' capabilities, often before they can see it for themselves.

We'll start with listening, as it's the foundation for everything that follows.

LISTENING

At its heart, compassionate leadership is about showing up for people in a human way – not just with good intentions, but with your full, generous attention. At the centre of this is how you listen.

Listening, done well, is one of the most powerful ways a leader can show people they matter. Yet, paradoxically, it's also one of the most overlooked. We often assume we're listening – but in reality, our minds are busy, our attention is split and we're already preparing what we'll say next.

Compassionate listening is different. It's not about nodding in the right places or waiting for your turn to speak. It's a deliberate, skilful act of generosity – giving someone the gift of your undivided attention and seeking to understand them more deeply.

When someone feels genuinely heard – fully, without judgement – something shifts. They feel safe. They open up. They begin to think more clearly, creatively and resourcefully. They often find courage they didn't know they had.

In our digital age, human attention has become a scarce and valuable resource. It is something that companies, platforms and creators actively compete for. Our time and focus are constantly pulled in a thousand directions – emails, meetings, notifications, endless demands on our bandwidth. In this environment, listening fully to another person has become a rare and valuable gift.

Below, we'll explore a framework for the four levels of listening. Each level has its place in leadership, but the most compassionate leaders learn to operate more consistently at the deeper levels – where listening becomes transformative.

Four levels of listening

As you read through these four levels of listening, imagine you are taking a lift downwards. You board the lift at Level 1, the surface level. With each level you descend, your listening deepens and widens, expanding to embrace your full capacity for noticing another person's experience.

Each level of listening has a particular mindset and purpose to anchor you there, supporting your role as a listener.

Level 1: Inward listening

Mindset: "What does this mean to me?"

Purpose: To interpret the world around you and identify your response to it.

Skillset: This is the most common kind of listening – and the level where most people spend most of their time. At Level 1, the spotlight of your attention is on yourself.

You hear the information the other person is sharing and immediately begin assessing what it means to you – how their words impact your own feelings, decisions and actions.

Listening at this level is, of course, essential in leadership. You need to gather data, feedback and perspectives to make good decisions. But it's not the kind of listening that builds trust or makes someone feel genuinely heard.

Example: A team member shares concerns about feeling overwhelmed. You hear them, but your mind quickly turns to how this will affect the delivery of next week's report.

You interrupt with, "Yes, I totally get it – I've been flat out too", and then shift the focus to timelines and expectations.

Insight: You've heard the words but filtered them through your own lens. Compassion was overtaken by urgency.

Tip: Notice when you're listening to respond or act, rather than listening to understand. If you're silently preparing your answer while the other person is still talking, you're probably at Level 1.

Level 2: Outward listening

Mindset: "What does this mean to you?"

Purpose: To clarify the other person's thoughts and your understanding of them.

Skillset: This is where compassionate listening starts to emerge. At Level 2, the spotlight of your attention shifts fully to the other person. You listen with your ears, your eyes and your voice:

- You hear their words while noticing the tone, pace and pitch of their speech – along with any pause or hesitation and what they leave unsaid.
- You observe their facial expressions, gestures, posture and movement.
- Occasionally, and without interpretation, you simply articulate what you notice or summarize what you've heard.

Through this simple act of witnessing and reflecting back, you allow the other person to hear themselves and see their situation more clearly.

Example: In a one-to-one meeting, a member of your team is updating you on a difficult client interaction. Whilst listening to their words, you notice that their typical enthusiasm is absent and their energy is very low. You reflect gently: "You've described how the conversation was very tense and uncomfortable – and now I'm noticing that your usual energy is missing. You appear very flat after this experience."

"I do feel flat", they reply with a sigh. "I think I'm just so disappointed that after all the work I put into this project, they would speak to me like that."

Insight: By paying attention to their words and non-verbal cues, you help them understand themselves more clearly – not fixing, just witnessing.

Tip: There can be a temptation to add value by interpreting or analysing – but that shifts the spotlight back onto you. Simply articulate what you heard or notice, allowing them to respond in their own way.

- "I notice you didn't finish what you were saying about your ambitions."
- "Your voice is very animated, and your eyes light up when you speak about the environment."
- "Let me check I've heard you correctly: you enjoy being in a position of responsibility, but only if you feel you have the necessary experience or expertise."
- "It sounds like you're clear on the long-term outcomes but are unsure of the next steps."

Level 3: Empathetic listening

Mindset: "How do you feel about this?"

Purpose: To deepen the other person's emotional awareness and support more accurate emotional labelling, bringing both of you greater insight and connection.

Skillset: At this level, you begin to tune into the emotional reality of the other person – not just what they're saying, but how they feel as they say it.

- You allow yourself to experience their energy, mood or story in your own body, noticing the feelings it stirs in you.
- You may occasionally name the emotions you sense, lightly and without needing to be right.
- You let them refine, reject or reshape your reflection as a way of deepening their own awareness.

Example: A junior manager confides in you after receiving tough feedback from a colleague. Giving them your full attention, you observe how they are speaking fast and loud, with high energy and plenty of hand gestures. They are very fired up and you sense anger and frustration in their account of the interaction. "It seems like receiving that feedback has made you quite angry."

Their energy level lowers a little as they reveal "I'm more frustrated than angry. Annoyed with myself for creating a situation that could have been avoided and letting other people down."

Insight: You've connected lightly with their emotional state. Your labelling and their re-labelling of their emotion gives them space to reflect and regulate.

Tip: Remain unattached to being "right", knowing that they may feel quite differently than you would in the same situation:

- "I sense that really hurt."
- "It feels like there's some worry or anxiety there."

Practising your emotional labelling skills (Chapter 6) will not only boost your own emotional awareness but also strengthen your ability to empathize with others.

Level 4: Intuitive listening

Mindset: "What is my intuition telling me about this person or situation?"

Purpose: To share intuitive insights that help the other person access their own inner wisdom.

Skillset: This is the most subtle and spacious level of listening. It involves trusting your inner wisdom – your sense of what might be happening, even if you can't explain it logically.

- You don't need to be right. You're simply offering a possibility.
- You allow the other person to accept, reject or reshape what you share.

Example: During a strategy session, a junior colleague seems upbeat and optimistic, but something feels off. You can't quite put your finger on it, but you sense a quiet tension. In a break, you gently say: "Can I check something with you? There's a part of me that senses you're uncomfortable or unsure about this approach – is that right?"

They pause, surprised – and then share: "There is something that's been niggling at me about the way we are tackling this – but I didn't want to seem negative." They go on to reveal a significant potential obstacle that no one else had considered.

Insight: You trusted your intuition and offered it lightly. The safe space you created gave them the courage to share a potentially unpopular thought.

Tip: Share your intuitive hunches as offerings, not conclusions:

- "Something about this makes me wonder..."
- "May I offer a thought that's come to me, even if I'm not sure why?

Improving your listening skills

However good you are at listening, you can always get better. I've been a professional listener for decades and have coached many leaders to listen more deeply – and I still find ways to improve. That's the joy of it. Each time you tune in just a little more fully, your ability to support others becomes more graceful, more effective and more impactful.

In my experience, most people underestimate the power of listening. With the best intentions, they rush to add value – offering solutions, ideas or fixes. Yet, sometimes, what's needed most is simple: to be heard.

Try this in your everyday conversations:

- **Level 1:** Notice when you're listening with your attention mainly on how what you're hearing affects you. Ask yourself: "What could I be missing here?"
- **Level 2:** Practise reflecting back only what you observe or hear – without judging, interpreting or fixing. Notice the impact this has on the other person and the quality of the conversation.

- **Level 3:** Experiment with lightly naming feelings – "I sense that...", "It feels like...". Notice how this deepens the exchange and what it adds to your relationship.
- **Level 4:** Share a quiet intuitive hunch and see what happens: "Can I share something that's just come to me?" Be willing to let it go if it doesn't resonate. It's all good practice.

Practise in everyday moments – at home, with your team, in the queue for coffee. Every time you listen more deeply, you strengthen your capacity to lead with presence and compassion.

Start small, go gently, and keep refining. Listening is a muscle – and every great leader I've ever coached is still building theirs.

CURIOSITY

Now that you've explored the simple but profound power of listening, let's layer in curiosity – the second practice of a compassionate leader.

When you intentionally add curiosity to your listening, you open the door to new understanding – not just for you, but for the other person too. Compassionate curiosity isn't just about gathering information for your own interest; it's about supporting someone else to explore their thoughts, feelings and actions more fully.

As leaders, there's often pressure to have the answers. But curious listening invites you to set that burden down. Instead of rushing to solve, you focus on asking the kinds of questions that unlock insight in others. It requires a subtle shift: stepping out of quick, efficient assessment and into a mindset of discovery. One that believes there is always something more to learn. Something deeper to uncover.

The curious mindset

Curiosity starts with openness. You let go of *knowing* and step into *not-knowing* – not as a weakness, but as a strength.

You believe that within every conversation lies the potential for:

- A deeper understanding.
- A stronger perspective.
- A new and more fruitful path forward.

This mindset will position you not as the expert with all the answers, but as a partner in exploration – walking alongside, not standing above.

The curious skillset

At the heart of compassionate curiosity is the ability to ask powerful questions that expand awareness and spark new thinking.

What makes a question powerful?

- It opens up rather than narrows down a conversation.
- It invites reflection, creativity and resourcefulness.
- It communicates belief in the other person's capacity to think for themselves.
- It's not designed to make you sound clever – it's designed to help them think more deeply.

Powerful questions tend to be:

- **Open:** Requiring more than a yes/no response.
- **Expansive:** Often starting with what, how, when or where.
- **Agenda-free:** Not steering toward the answer you want.
- **Short and simple:** Sparking thought, not stealing focus.

For example:

- "What do you need right now?"
- "How do you feel about that?"
- "Where might you find the answer?"
- "When will you know it's time?"
- "What's most important?"

Questions that are leading, loaded or make the other person feel defensive tend to close a conversation down, eroding the trust that is needed to reflect more deeply and speak freely.

Here are a few examples of questions that sound curious, but communicate a hidden agenda:

- "Do you think you'd like to get more involved in the operational side of the business?"
- "Why did you choose that approach to such a complex, politically sensitive assignment?"
- "Is the idea of transferring to a different team appealing to you?"
- "After all the time we've invested in developing you for this role, where do you see your future heading?"

The difference is subtle but significant. Powerful questions invite expansion; weaker questions tend to close things down, add pressure or guide someone toward your preferred answer.

Tip: Avoid starting questions with "Why...". Even with the best intentions, "why" often feels like "justify yourself", triggering defensiveness rather than openness. Instead, try framing the same curiosity with what, how, or when.

Staying curious as you listen

Compassionate curiosity doesn't stop when you've asked the question. Stay present and hold your attention as they respond. Every interjection you make shapes the conversation – so notice their words, tone, posture and energy. Adjust your pace, your tone and your next question accordingly.

This is Graceful Power – not controlling the conversation, but helping something deeper, more authentic and ultimately more helpful, unfold.

BELIEF IN POTENTIAL

The third practice of compassionate leadership is the belief in potential – your willingness to see beyond current performance and hold a bigger vision for what someone can become. This isn't blind optimism or naïve hope. It's a deliberate choice to look for untapped capability and to create the conditions where it can flourish.

With compassion, a leader with Graceful Power recognizes present reality but also invests in possibility – especially when someone can't yet see it for themselves.

Case study: Bill Holroyd – the power of believing in potential

With characteristic understatement, Bill Holroyd told me, "I do find it hard to see the bad in people."

More accurately, Bill has spent his life choosing to see the best in people – and it's a choice that has served him remarkably well. "I can't think of any time this approach has gone wrong", he says. "Things may not always have worked out as planned, but it's been a good policy for life."

From a young age, Bill questioned rules and expected ways of doing things that didn't seem to serve a purpose. That independent streak got him expelled from school – but it also laid the foundations for doing things differently. He went on to build two national foodservice distribution networks: first for the Forte Group, and later his own business, Holroyd Meek, which he built from scratch and sold in 1995.

The proceeds from that sale allowed Bill to scale his instinct for spotting potential beyond traditional business. He became a serial investor – often backing people with bright ideas but without the conventional track record most investors would demand.

One investment in particular tested his resolve. The early years were rocky, with multiple setbacks that would have sent many investors running. But Bill remained loyal. He saw something in the founder that others had missed. His continued support – financial and personal – eventually paid off. That venture became his most successful by far, and the founder credits Bill's steadfast belief as pivotal to their journey.

Bill's belief in people doesn't stop at business. It fuels what he considers his proudest achievement: the creation of the charity OnSide. OnSide Youth Zones are a network of state-of-the-art facilities for young people in some of the UK's most economically disadvantaged communities. Inside these incredible spaces, skilled and committed youth workers help young people see what they're capable of – and give them the tools and confidence to pursue it.

The vision is growing. Bill hopes to see many more Youth Zones established across the UK, expanding the reach of this powerful model of belief and support.

I was introduced to Bill during the research for this book as "the person who gets people to work harder than they've ever worked before – in the nicest possible way." It's a fitting description. His ability to draw out extraordinary effort and ambition in others comes not from pressure, but from belief. People want to rise to the potential he sees in them.

Bill Holroyd's leadership shows us that believing in people isn't naïve – it's catalytic. His ability to trust, support and expect more from others has created financial success, social impact and a legacy of empowered lives.

Believing in potential – even when it's hard

It's easy to believe in someone when they're performing well, fit seamlessly into the team culture and are fully aligned with the organization's purpose. But what about when that isn't the case?

A compassionate leader with Graceful Power recognizes that belief matters even more when someone is struggling – especially when they've stopped believing in themselves.

Sometimes, though, belief means recognizing that a person's potential may unfold *somewhere else*. When a new hire joins your team, both of you are full of hope. But sometimes, despite encouragement, guidance and goodwill, it becomes clear they're not the right fit. It might be that they were never suited to the role, that the organization has changed around them, or that their aspirations will be better served elsewhere.

Too often, people in this situation are labelled "a problem". They feel criticized, sidelined and unvalued. A leader with Graceful Power takes a different approach: holding belief in someone's broader potential, even if the best way to unlock it is helping them transition into a different environment.

Case study: Julia Ingall – seeing the potential beyond the problem

Julia Ingall, a seasoned Chief People Officer, has faced this dilemma many times. She recalls one young man in particular – let's call him Dan.

Dan had talent and delivered results. But his communication style created tension with his manager and teammates, and he lacked the self-awareness to realize that his own behaviour was holding him back. Despite coaching, direct conversations and formal warnings, the time came when Dan had to be let go.

Julia felt saddened by this outcome. She saw real potential in Dan – potential that risked going to waste, not because of his skills, but because of how he was choosing to show up.

After the formal meeting, Julia took a risk. She asked Dan to stay behind. Gently but firmly, she said:

> "Listen, I know today feels tough. I know you didn't want to lose this job. But this could be a defining moment in your career – if you choose to let it be. You have real talent..." *(and here she named his specific skills and strengths)* "...but your approach has been holding you back. We gave you warnings, but they didn't shift things. Maybe this shock will. I believe in your potential. I believe you can grow from this and go on to

do great things, if you can find the courage to learn from this. If I can support you in the next few months, you know where I am."

A few days later, Julia received an email. Dan thanked her for that conversation – for holding belief in him, even when he couldn't see it himself.

Julia had to let Dan go. The needs of the business required it. But she did so with courage, congruence and compassion – showing him he still mattered, and she still believed in who he could become.

Three practices for demonstrating belief

The *mindset* behind believing in potential is simple but profound: you hold steady faith in a person's capacity to grow, even when it's not obvious, even when they can't see it themselves. This mindset is rooted in sincere respect for people and a belief in what's possible.

The *skillset* is how you express that mindset in practice. In leadership, it shows up most powerfully through three consistent behaviours:

1. **Recognition:** Affirming who a person is *being*, not just what they are *doing*.
2. **Championing:** Naming and amplifying the potential you see in others, especially when their self-belief is low.
3. **Growth-oriented feedback:** Offering feedback designed to support development and stretch someone's capabilities, not simply correct performance.

Let's explore these three leadership skills in more detail.

1. Recognition

Offering recognition of who someone is *being* – beyond what they are doing – is a powerful and often overlooked leadership skill.

Many leaders are comfortable expressing gratitude for strong results or praising performance, and these acknowledgements matter.

But recognizing the *admirable qualities* someone brings to their work – regardless of the outcome – takes leadership to the next level.

For example:

- "Reuben, your determination in creating this conference really shone through this week."
- "Younas, you were calm and wise during this morning's crisis with the sound system."
- "Audrey, you have an infectious enthusiasm that lifts everyone's spirits."
- "Fran, you showed real courage in handling our keynote speaker."

At first, this practice can feel uncomfortable. In leadership workshops, when I encourage participants to try acknowledging each other in this way, the room fills with nervous tension. Yet afterwards, the atmosphere softens as people connect and relate to each other differently.

When you pause to recognize the human qualities someone brings to their work – not just their output – the effect on both you and them can be transformative.

2. *Championing*

While recognition affirms who someone *is*, championing is about who they *can become*.

Championing means actively naming the potential you see in others – especially when their own self-belief is faltering. It helps people see beyond their current limitations and access their greater capabilities.

For example:

- "I can see you leading a project of this scale in the future – you have a natural clarity and presence when speaking to groups."
- "You have a real talent for navigating tough conversations with empathy. I see you playing a crucial role in our team dynamics."

- "With your creative thinking and determination, you have the potential to drive significant innovation in our organization."

Championing potential not only strengthens others' confidence, but also deepens your leadership influence. By believing in and advocating for potential, you foster motivation, resilience and a powerful culture of growth and support.

Recognition vs. championing: Two distinct but related skills

There are similarities between the skills of recognition and championing – yet each has a distinct role, bringing subtle differences.

Practised together, they create a powerful balance of belonging and growth: "I see you as you are today – and I believe in who you can become."

	Recognition	**Championing**
Purpose	Celebrates who someone is being right now – affirming their qualities, presence and contribution.	Amplifies who they are becoming – expressing belief in their future possibilities and untapped potential.
Authenticity	Recognition must be genuine and specific to the individual to avoid feeling superficial or manipulative.	Champion only what you truly believe is achievable. Sincerity builds trust and strengthens confidence.
Observation	Pay close attention to the person's behaviours, attitudes and interactions so your recognition is grounded in reality.	Connect your belief in their potential to observable strengths and tangible examples, making your championing credible.

	Recognition	Championing
Timing	Offer recognition promptly, soon after noticing an admirable quality or behaviour, to reinforce and celebrate it.	Champion potential at key moments – after setbacks, during new challenges or when confidence falters – so your belief carries greater impact.
Personalization	Tailor your recognition to the individual's unique strengths or traits so they feel deeply seen and valued.	Align your championing with their personal aspirations and values to make your support meaningful and motivating.
Directness	Express recognition to the person directly; speaking about their qualities to others has less impact.	Be clear and direct when expressing your belief in their future potential, making your confidence in them unmistakable.

3. *Growth-oriented feedback*

I love planting acorns. It never ceases to amaze me that inside those small, warm brown seeds lies the potential for a mighty oak – a tree that could stand for centuries, supporting a thriving ecosystem hosting hundreds of other species. My role in that extraordinary journey is simple but significant: to germinate the seeds, nurture the saplings, protect them from harm and give them what they need to flourish. I believe in their potential and nurture it – even though I won't be around to witness the magnificent trees they'll one day become.

Growth-oriented feedback calls for the same mindset: Holding a vision of someone's future potential while focusing on what they need right now to grow. Every piece of feedback becomes nourishment, supporting the person to flourish.

Common pitfalls

Handled well, feedback can be a powerful opportunity to connect deeply with your team. Done badly, it risks undermining trust and motivation. Even well-intentioned feedback often falls into these traps:

- **The feedback dump:** Saving up all the feedback for one big, overwhelming session, leaving recipients blindsided or discouraged.
- **Vague praise, specific critique:** A pattern where positive feedback is general ("You're doing fine") but criticism is highly detailed – creating an unbalanced and demotivating experience.
- **Feedback-as-fact:** Presenting subjective opinions as if universally true, shutting down meaningful dialogue (e.g., "You're not a team player" rather than "I've noticed a few moments where collaboration has been tricky").
- **The "compliment sandwich":** Criticism routinely sandwiched between two pieces of praise, which dilutes authenticity and often feels manipulative.
- **"Constructive feedback":** Often a euphemism for criticism in disguise, especially when not genuinely helpful or actionable.

The generous gift of feedback

Leaders with Graceful Power avoid the common pitfalls of feedback by holding a simple but powerful mindset: everyone has the ability to grow when the right conditions are created.

Think of feedback as a gift – an act of generosity offered in service of the other person's development, not as a judgement or a test. Before you speak, pause and ask yourself: "What does this person need to hear right now to thrive and move closer to their greater potential?"

Use these prompts to prepare and time your feedback effectively:

- **Daily:** "What are they doing particularly well that they should keep doing?"
- **Regularly:** "What do they do occasionally that, if done more consistently, would significantly improve their performance?"
- **Rarely:** "What behaviour is holding them back – and needs to stop?"

Guidelines for giving feedback with Graceful Power:

- Be clear and straightforward – avoid jargon, euphemisms or vague statements.
- Integrate recognition and championing so your feedback connects to the person's qualities and potential, not just their performance.
- Choose your timing carefully – offer feedback as close as possible to the moment, while being mindful of the environment and who else is present.
- Match the weight of the feedback to the moment – a brief comment when that's all that's needed; a deeper, more thoughtful conversation when the situation calls for it.

When offered with care, clarity and compassion, feedback becomes more than correction – it becomes encouragement. It tells people you see them, you believe in them and you're invested in helping them grow.

Feedback vs. formal performance conversations

Feedback is not the same as addressing chronic underperformance. If someone repeatedly falls short despite supportive coaching, it calls for a different type of conversation: one that's structured, formal and focused on corrective action.

Everyday feedback, by contrast, is about course-correction and growth in the moment – offering small, real-time insights before challenges escalate into patterns.

Case study: Kofi Amoo-Gottfried – clear and kind

One of the paradoxes of modern leadership is that the more deeply you care about your people, the more often you'll need to have hard conversations with them. When you care, it's natural to want to spare someone's feelings – yet avoiding a difficult truth can quietly become an act of self-protection rather than genuine support.

Kofi Amoo-Gottfried, now Chief Marketing Officer at DoorDash, remembers wrestling with this early in his leadership journey. During one of our coaching conversations, we talked about his discomfort with wielding power.

Raised in Ghana, Kofi grew up in a culture where hierarchy was deeply embedded – where elders were revered and questioning authority wasn't encouraged. That experience left him, as he puts it, with a lifelong aversion to authoritative power. "The worst way to approach me", he says, "is to tell me I have to do something – I'm most likely to do the exact opposite!"

As Kofi moved into senior leadership roles in some of the world's most influential companies, he realized he needed to find a new relationship with power – one that didn't betray his values but honoured them. He wanted to lead powerfully while staying true to himself.

One insight from our early coaching work stayed with him: avoiding hard truths is not compassion. When we withhold honest feedback – especially when it could help someone grow – we deny them the chance to learn, adapt and succeed.

Kofi began to see that naming the hard thing, with care and clarity, was not just a courageous act – it was a deeply kind one.

He now describes his approach to leadership like this: "How can I use the position I'm in to unlock the magic in someone else? How do I create opportunities? How do I see things in them that maybe they don't yet see – or the organization doesn't see – and give them the belief they can get to the next place?"

He adds: "Sometimes that requires an uncomfortable conversation for both of us. And sometimes, it means the place they'll progress isn't here – it's not in this team or this company."

Kofi learned to use his power in a way that felt authentic: courageous enough to face discomfort, compassionate enough to act in the best interests of someone's future potential – not just their current role.

Brené Brown captures this beautifully in her book *Dare to Lead*:[1] "Clear is kind. Unclear is unkind."

She writes:

> "Feeding people half-truths or bullshit to make them feel better (which is almost always about making ourselves feel more comfortable) is unkind. Not getting clear with a colleague about your expectations because it feels too hard, yet holding them accountable or blaming them for not delivering, is unkind. Talking about people rather than to them is unkind."

I couldn't agree more.

Having the courage to be clear with someone is an act of deep respect. It demonstrates your belief in their potential and your willingness to sit in the discomfort required to help them achieve it.

For Kofi, the challenge was giving feedback on performance or helping someone face the reality that they might not be the right fit for the team or organization. For you, the edge may lie somewhere else – offering genuine praise, naming someone's personal strengths or entrusting them with a challenging assignment.

Whatever it is for you, choose the courageous path: be even more kind, even more compassionate. Say what they need to hear, not just what's easiest to say.

Honing your compassion

The practices we've explored in this chapter – listening deeply, being curious and believing in the potential of others – are simple in principle but profound in impact. Together, they form the mindset and skillset of compassionate leadership.

Compassion in the context of Graceful Power isn't about being soft or endlessly agreeable. It's about being fully present with the people you lead, creating space for them to be seen, heard and supported. When you listen generously, you make people feel valued. When you stay curious, you uncover insights that surface only when someone feels truly understood. When you consistently communicate your belief in their potential, you give people permission to see more in themselves than they might have thought possible.

Exercise: Reflection and action

Take a few minutes to pause and reflect on the three practices you've explored in this chapter:

1. **Listening:** How often do you listen at Levels 2, 3 or 4 – fully and beyond your own perspective?
2. **Curiosity:** When and with who could you ask more powerful, open questions that help someone see a situation differently?
3. **Belief in potential:** Who around you would benefit from hearing your recognition, championing or feedback for their growth?

Over the next week, choose two conversations where you consciously practise all three skills:

- Bring your full attention – listen not just to the words, but also to the pauses, emotions and unspoken cues.
- Ask powerful questions that invite deeper reflection rather than supplying your own thoughts.
- Before ending the conversation, affirm something you see in them – a strength, a quality or a glimpse of potential they may

not fully recognize themselves. Give feedback that encourages them to lean into this strength, quality or potential even further.

Notice what happens – not just in them, but in you.

Compassionate leadership begins one conversation at a time, but its influence reaches much further. When leaders practise these skills consistently, they create the conditions where people feel safe, valued and inspired to contribute at their best.

In the next chapter, we'll zoom out from individual relationships to the broader climate you're creating as a leader. We'll explore how to shape an environment where people and performance flourish together – where compassion isn't just something you practise one-on-one, but something that becomes embedded in the way your whole team or organization works.

Chapter 12

Creating a climate of flourishing

Leaders with Graceful Power understand that compassion isn't something reserved for moments of crisis – it's something they intentionally weave into the fabric of everyday leadership. They don't just react when people struggle; they design environments where people can thrive. These leaders cultivate teams where motivation, wellbeing and performance are not competing priorities, but interconnected outcomes.

When we create climates of flourishing, we're not aiming to remove difficulty from the workplace, but to give people the emotional and structural conditions that help them navigate challenging times. The most powerful environments are not those that push people to their limits, but those that help people expand their limits without burning out.

In this chapter, we'll explore four practical dimensions of compassionate leadership that enable leaders to create these conditions:

- **Team culture:** Shaping the environment people experience every day.
- **Meeting individual needs:** Recognizing and responding to differences with care.
- **Professional growth and progression:** Unlocking potential and championing possibility.

- **Connection to mission and purpose:** Inspiring people with meaning and direction.

Team culture

Culture can be easy to overlook – until it starts to feel uncomfortable, exclude people or wear them down. Culture is the atmosphere we breathe at work – the unwritten rules, the way meetings feel, who speaks up and who stays quiet. Leaders with Graceful Power don't leave the culture of their team or organization to develop by chance. They intentionally and compassionately shape the dynamics and working environment.

A foundation of behavioural norms built around shared values and respect fosters psychological safety. This encourages team members to share new ideas, admit mistakes or challenge assumptions without fear of embarrassment or negative consequences. Harvard Business School professor, Amy Edmondson,[1] defines psychological safety as a "shared belief held by members of a team that the team is safe for interpersonal risk-taking". When this kind of safety exists, teams don't avoid hard things – they're simply more willing to face them together.

Google's Project Aristotle,[2] which studied high-performing teams, found psychological safety to be the single most important factor distinguishing effective teams from the rest. Without it, collaboration falters and creativity declines. With it, people contribute more openly, innovate more freely and grow in confidence and capability.

Boundaries are another key element of compassionate team culture. These include practical norms around working hours, messaging habits and time off – but also emotional boundaries. Leaders must be clear about what behaviour supports the culture they want to create and be willing to step in when lines are crossed.

Modelling self-care is just as important. If leaders regularly burn the candle at both ends, answer emails late at night or wear exhaustion as a badge of honour, their teams will assume that's what's expected. By setting self-respecting boundaries for themselves, leaders give permission for others to do the same.

Case study: Rebecca Van Dyck – creating the conditions for people to thrive

Rebecca Van Dyck draws on her background in sport to inform her approach to leadership. As a member of a US college soccer team, she experienced a culture where each player was encouraged not only to "know their weaknesses and play to their strengths" but also to take collective responsibility for helping one another succeed. Team members covered for each other without judgement – an ethos of mutual respect and psychological safety that left a lasting impression.

Rebecca carried this mindset into her role as a marketing leader, choosing to create environments where people feel safe enough to take risks in pursuit of stronger, more creative outcomes. She pays close attention to what her people need to flourish and then acts on it. She communicates her expectations clearly and consistently – and most powerfully through her own behaviour. When she asks her team to honour a certain way of working or treating one another, she models it herself, earning the right to hold others accountable when they fall outside the agreed cultural norms.

When we spoke, Rebecca told me how her compassionate, culture-building leadership was tested during her early years at Facebook, where she led the company's first foray into marketing. Despite a talented team and the supportive environment she had nurtured, they experienced what Rebecca openly calls "epic failures" as they worked to define an effective strategy. These failures were highly visible, intensely scrutinized and widely criticized across the organization, with feedback arriving relentlessly, often at all hours.

Rebecca remained steadfast in her belief in the team's potential – if given the right conditions to succeed. She adapted the climate around them, protecting their capacity to do great work. She acted as a buffer, absorbing unproductive criticism and translating the rest into constructive insight they could actually use. She also tightened boundaries to maintain clarity and calm. For example, while they couldn't control when emails arrived from the wider organization, she insisted that the team avoid emailing each other after hours or at weekends. Everyone deserved time to decompress. Crucially, she modelled this behaviour herself, sending a powerful signal: this is how we do things around here.

Even in the thick of challenge, Rebecca helped her team maintain perspective. She acknowledged the pressure but reminded them it would pass, expressed her belief in their ability to succeed, and reframed the situation as a valuable stretch in their careers – something they would one day look back on as formative.

The impact of her leadership extended beyond her immediate team. As word spread about the culture she had created, people from other departments began requesting to join.

Rebecca's Graceful Power is defined by her compassionate awareness of what her people need, her courageous determination to meet those needs and the congruence between what she says and what she does. Her story shows us that great leaders don't just focus on performance – they create the conditions that make high performance possible. Through attentive leadership, clear boundaries and behavioural consistency, Rebecca demonstrates how to build a thriving, high-performing team culture – even under intense pressure.

Reflection

Rebecca's example is inspiring, but it's also achievable. You don't need a Facebook-sized team or a Silicon Valley budget to build a thriving culture – you need to lead attentively, behave with consistency and practise courageous care.

Take a moment to reflect on your own team culture:

- How would your people describe "the way we do things around here"?
- Do they feel safe to speak up, share ideas and admit mistakes without fear of judgement?
- Are you modelling the boundaries and behaviours you want to see in your team?
- What small actions could you take this week and next – in your words, behaviour or expectations – to make your team's environment more supportive, open and thriving?

MEETING INDIVIDUAL NEEDS

Compassionate leaders recognize that while people may work as a team, no two individuals experience that work in quite the same way. Our different backgrounds, strengths and circumstances shape what we need in order to perform at our best – and leaders who understand this create environments where everyone has the opportunity to thrive.

It's less about labels and more about removing unnecessary barriers. This means noticing when people need different kinds of support and making adjustments where possible, so that everyone has access to the resources and opportunities they need to do their best work.

Sometimes these needs are enduring – shaped by how we process information, manage energy or balance personal commitments. At other times, they're temporary: a team member navigating bereavement, returning from parental leave or going through a major life change. Graceful Power means responding thoughtfully to these different needs with curiosity, flexibility and practical care.

Adjustments should be normalized, not exceptional. That might mean offering flexibility around working hours, providing information in different formats or giving someone time to rebuild confidence after a significant transition. When leaders weave these considerations into the culture rather than treating them as one-off favours, they send a powerful signal: everyone is valued and supported.

Case study: Meeting needs, unlocking strength

I recently heard this story about Alex, a talented analyst who had begun to wonder whether the differences they noticed in their working style, compared with others, might be linked to ADHD. With professional support, that exploration led to a formal diagnosis. It helped explain why Alex had been feeling increasingly sidelined and criticized: their previous manager had read missed deadlines as a lack of commitment and stopped offering stretching projects.

Somewhat trepidatiously, Alex approached their new team leader – and was relieved to find him warm, open and curious about how to help

Alex do their best work. Together they made a few practical adjustments to how work was planned and prioritized – shorter sprints, a shared calendar and a peer buddy for collaborative planning – and they looked at how to make the most of Alex's strengths. The leader began to involve Alex in complex, cross-team questions where holding multiple perspectives is useful, asked them to lead problem-solving discussions and gave them space to bring their positive energy to early idea-shaping.

Within weeks, Alex's confidence and contributions flourished – along with their loyalty and commitment to their new boss. Their experience shows the impact leaders can have when they listen without judgement and adapt thoughtfully, meeting individual needs to create a climate where everyone can flourish.

Reflection

Take a moment to reflect on how confident you are that everyone in your team has what they need to succeed:

- Do you have a clear understanding of the different needs, working styles and strengths of the people you lead?
- Are there hidden barriers – in your systems, expectations or culture – that might be limiting someone's contribution?
- How do you signal, through your words and actions, that everyone deserves the resources and opportunities they need to thrive?
- Whose guidance or support can you seek to ensure you are meeting the differing needs of your team?

PROFESSIONAL GROWTH AND PROGRESSION

Leaders with Graceful Power use their compassion not only to measure what people deliver, but to nurture who they are becoming. Compassion in this context means paying close attention to each person's growth – understanding what they need to stretch, succeed and stay motivated – and championing the potential you see in them.

People flourish when they feel they're learning and moving forward, stretching into their potential rather than stuck in a holding pattern. This isn't simply about training courses or formal development plans. The most powerful growth often happens in the flow of work itself – through stretch assignments, collaborative projects, mentoring or moments when someone believes in you enough to say: "I know you can do this."

When leaders combine a compassionate mindset with practical skill – listening, being curious, noticing strengths and providing both challenge and support – they create the conditions for growth that transform individuals, teams and organizations.

Case Study: Carter Murray – championing growth

Carter Murray's superpower has always been his immense energy and drive. In his early career, he often relied on this strength to win people over through sheer force of personality. He tells me how an insight shared by one client in particular – that his boundless enthusiasm could sometimes overpower even the most senior people in the room – prompted Carter to pause and reflect. It inspired him not to hold back his energy, but to expand his approach, channelling his enthusiasm more thoughtfully and strategically.

Today, Carter leads by the mantra: "Seek first to understand, then to be understood." He combines his natural energy with a genuine curiosity about others – listening carefully to what excites and drains people and exploring their dreams and ambitions. These insights allow him to tailor his message and channel his enthusiasm in ways that resonate most powerfully with each individual. He confidently articulates the potential he sees and creates environments where people can stretch beyond even their own expectations. For many, this combination – being seen clearly, believed in deeply and given the conditions to succeed – has been transformational.

This approach was never more valuable than during Carter's tenure as Global CEO of FCB, then one of the world's largest communications groups. Tasked with revitalizing the network's fortunes and reputation, Carter knew that success depended on attracting the best creative talent and helping them shine. By taking the time to listen and understand what motivated people, he was able to promise – and deliver – the conditions they needed to thrive. He recruited ambitious, high-potential people from FCB's competitors and championed their growth relentlessly, coaching and supporting them to achieve more than they thought possible.

The results spoke for themselves: under Carter's leadership, FCB experienced one of the most successful periods in its history – a testament to the power of combining energy, belief and compassion to unlock both people's potential and an organization's success.

Case Study: Kofi Amoo-Gottfried – leading growth for all

Kofi Amoo-Gottfried, Chief Marketing Officer at DoorDash, models his belief in continuing professional development by sharing his annual performance review openly with his team. He talks about where he plans to focus his development and the feedback he's acting on. This transparent approach inspires his team to take ownership of their own growth more powerfully than words of encouragement ever could – and it earns their deep respect.

In the same spirit, Kofi also expects his leaders to be just as skilled at "raising the floor" as they are at "raising the ceiling". By raising the ceiling, he means helping high performers stretch further from a place of strength – often the easier part of leadership. Raising the floor, however, takes greater care and commitment: it's about working thoughtfully with those who are struggling, helping them build the skills and confidence they need to contribute at their best.

Carter and Kofi illustrate two essential facets of leadership with Graceful Power:

1. **Seeing and believing in potential:** Unlocking growth through deep listening, curiosity, and championing others.
2. **Balancing stretch and support:** Creating the conditions where people feel safe enough to take risks and equipped to succeed.

Leaders who practise these qualities don't just grow performance – they grow people.

Reflection

Take a moment to reflect on how you support the growth of those you lead:

- Do you know the personal ambitions, strengths and aspirations of each member of your team?
- How confident are you that their development opportunities align with what matters most to them?
- Are you balancing challenge with support, giving people both the stretch and safety they need to grow?
- Revisit your reflections on your *Bad Boss* and your *Great Boss* from Chapter 10. If you were to reprioritize some of your time to focus on being more like the latter, what differences would your team notice?

CONNECTION TO MISSION AND PURPOSE

Leaders with Graceful Power use their compassion to keep people connected to why their work matters. They recognize that meaning fuels motivation: when people believe their personal mission or ambitions align with those of their team and organization, they bring more energy, creativity and commitment to their work.

Leaders play a vital role in helping their teams build and sustain this aligned sense of purpose. They make the bigger picture visible – regularly articulating what the organization is striving towards, showing how each person's contribution matters, celebrating progress and naming the difference the team is making.

Keeping purpose alive

Consider Clare Hornby, founder of the fashion brand Me+Em, who we met in Chapter 6. Every month, she personally reminds every employee of the company's mission and the strategy to achieve it. Her goal is simple but significant: to ensure everyone feels connected to the central purpose of the business and energized by the part they play in making it happen.

People can tolerate extraordinary complexity and challenge if they believe their work has meaning. But in high-pressure or fast-moving environments, that sense of meaning can be fragile – easily lost in the churn of deadlines, crises and competing demands.

During the intensely challenging period at Facebook, shared earlier in this chapter, Rebecca Van Dyck kept her creative teams focused by repeatedly connecting today's trials with their longer-term ambitions. She reminded them that every idea, even those rejected internally, expanded their personal portfolios. She reframed setbacks as investments in their bank of experience and reminded them that the resilience they were building would benefit their long-term careers. By holding the team's attention on a shared vision of success – while respecting each person's individual motivations – Rebecca kept people energized, confident and committed through turbulent times.

Case study: Simon Casson – immersing people in purpose

Simon Casson, now CEO of the Corinthia Hotels Group and formerly President of Four Seasons Hotels, understands that a luxury experience isn't defined by decor, but by people. With a lifetime in hospitality, he knows that the most lasting impression guests take away is the warmth, attentiveness and skill of the people who serve them.

Simon leads with kindness and respect, while also being relentless in his pursuit of excellence. He continually reminds every member of his team – through both his words and his actions – of the critical role they play in delivering world-class experiences.

When launching the Four Seasons Hotel in Doha, Simon tells me how he led the recruitment of 600 new team members from around the world. Determined to embed the company's values from day one, he personally conducted every single final interview. As the new recruits arrived in Doha, they were met at the airport by someone holding a sign with their name, welcomed with a personal letter from Simon, and provided with meticulously prepared accommodation, uniforms and induction plans.

This wasn't just onboarding – it was immersion. From the moment they arrived, every employee experienced the company's people-focused ethos in action: kindness, respect, attention to detail and the relentless pursuit of excellence. While each individual had their own reasons for joining – new opportunities, financial security, professional growth – Simon's compassionate leadership united them behind a shared mission and a collective purpose.

Tapping into shared and individual motivators

When leaders want to inspire and energize their people – or bring life back to a team that has lost its conviction – there's a natural tendency to appeal to the drivers they themselves find motivating. Sometimes this works, but often it falls flat because people are driven by different things.

A more thoughtful and effective approach begins with curiosity: listening deeply to your team, understanding what excites them, what drains them and what they aspire to achieve. When you know what matters most to each individual, you can tailor your words and actions to connect their personal drivers with the team's shared purpose.

The following scenario uses the nine sources of motivation introduced in Chapter 5 to illustrate how a leader might re-energize a team after a setback.

Scenario: Rebuilding energy after a setback

A cross-functional team has been working for months on a high-profile product launch. Despite their commitment and hard work, the launch is delayed due to external factors outside their control – a supplier failure and unexpected regulatory challenges. The delay means missed revenue targets and visible disappointment from senior leadership. Morale dips and confidence falters. People feel tired, frustrated and uncertain about what comes next.

Sensing the exhaustion, the team leader brings everyone together for a reset. The goal isn't just to debrief the setback but to rebuild energy and reconnect the team with their sense of meaning and purpose. She prepares her message carefully, speaking to the different motivators she knows are present within the group:

- **Expertise:** "There are real learnings for us here that we can apply going forward – I'll be asking for your insight to shape how we improve our launch framework across the business."
- **Relationships:** "We've been through this together and I'm proud of the way we've supported each other – let's keep that trust at the heart of how we move forward."
- **Recognition:** "Your effort in this project has not gone unnoticed – I'll be spotlighting our team's resilience and innovation in next week's leadership offsite."
- **Responsibility:** "This is a moment to lead from the front – I'm giving you ownership of the revised strategy stream and I trust your judgement to steer it."
- **Tangible reward:** "We've reworked the delivery plan to protect bonus eligibility and reward targets – I'll keep you informed and ensure your hard work leads to tangible outcomes."
- **Impact:** "This setback doesn't change the value of what we're doing – we're still building something that will genuinely improve people's lives."
- **Innovation:** "We've got a rare chance to rethink how this could be even better – if you have creative ideas, now is the time to bring them forward."

- **Stability:** "Here's what we're doing to stabilize the timeline and reduce future risk – and why your role is key to bringing calm and control back into the picture."
- **Independence:** "Structure is important, but I want to give you flexibility in how you tackle the next phase – if you see a better way, run with it."

In this scenario, the leader demonstrates compassion, clarity and strategic awareness. By recognizing her team's emotional state and appealing to what personally drives each individual, she rebuilds energy, restores alignment and moves the team forward together.

Reflection

Notice the regularity and consistency with which Clare Hornby, Rebecca van Dyck and Simon Casson communicate the mission of the business to their people, enrolling them individually and collectively into a shared sense of purpose.

- How often do you communicate the bigger picture behind your team's work?
- Do your people understand how their individual contributions make a difference to the organization's mission?
- Are you attuned to the different motivators driving your team members, or are you assuming they're similar to your own?
- When energy or momentum dips, what steps could you take to reconnect your team with their sense of purpose and re-ignite their motivation?

THE FLOURISHING CHECKLIST

The practices you've explored in this chapter – shaping team culture, meeting individual needs, supporting growth and connection to purpose – are at the heart of creating a climate where people thrive. But flourishing doesn't happen by accident. It requires conscious, ongoing attention.

Use the questions below to assess the current climate within your team. You might choose to answer them privately first and then share them with your team for an open discussion about where you're thriving – and where there's room to grow together.

Team culture

- Do people feel safe to speak up, ask questions and take thoughtful risks?
- Are there clear boundaries around time, communication and wellbeing?
- Do I consistently model the culture I want others to live?

Meeting individual needs

- Do I understand the experiences and circumstances shaping my team members' needs?
- Are adjustments and flexibility built into the culture – or treated as rare exceptions?
- Do people feel equally seen, supported and valued for who they are as well as what they deliver?

Professional growth and progression

- Are we investing in people's development, not just their output?
- Do I balance challenge with support, giving people both stretch and safety?
- Do I actively nurture the potential of others through recognition, championing and feedback?

Purpose and vision

- Do we regularly talk about why our work matters – beyond the tasks and targets?

- Do we celebrate meaningful progress, not just big wins?
- Do people feel connected to a shared sense of purpose that inspires and sustains them?

Flourishing is never a one-time achievement; you have to keep adjusting and investing. Use this checklist as a regular touchpoint – for yourself and your team – to keep your culture intentional, your leadership aligned and your people thriving.

Compassion in leadership is often misunderstood as "soft". What you've seen throughout this part of the book is that, far from being passive or permissive, compassion is a powerful driver of performance, belonging and human potential. It's about noticing what people need – to feel safe, to feel seen and to feel capable of growth – and responding with intention.

You've explored how leaders with Graceful Power cultivate compassion through practice:

- **Listening deeply:** Tuning into more than words to understand what's really being said.
- **Leading with curiosity:** Seeking to understand before being understood.
- **Believing in potential:** Recognizing, championing and unlocking the talent in others.
- **Creating climates of flourishing:** Where culture, care, growth and purpose intertwine.

We reviewed how the importance of self-compassion mustn't be overlooked. To sustain yourself – and to be able to offer genuine care to others – you need the same kindness, patience and respect for your own limits that you aim to extend to your team. This isn't indulgence; it's responsible leadership.

These compassion practices, alongside congruence and courage, work together to build Graceful Power. As we move into the final part of this book, we'll bring these threads together. You'll see how congruence, courage and compassion combine to create a leadership presence that is grounded and bold, steady and adaptable, human and high-performing.

PART V

LEADING WITH GRACEFUL POWER

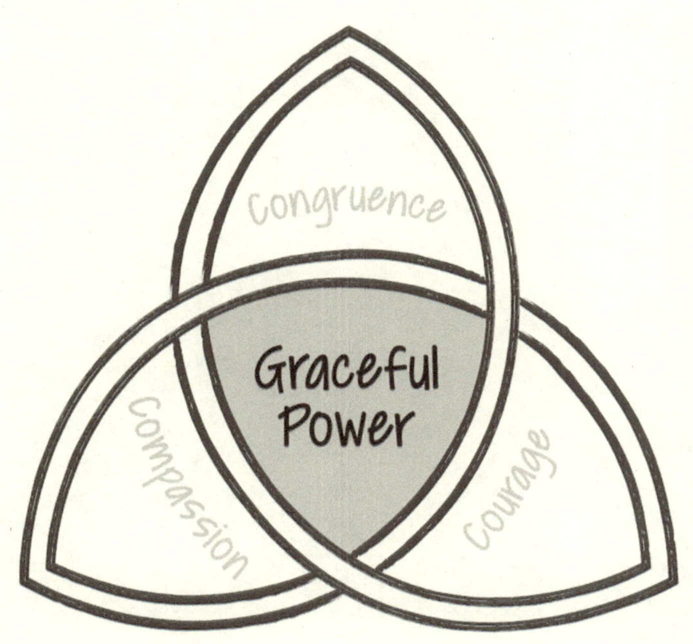

Chapter 13

Bringing it all together

By this point, you will have built a strong foundation for your Graceful Power.

You've explored congruence and created your Code of Congruence – a living reminder of:

- The values you choose to honour.
- The wiser leader you are becoming.
- The leadership style that is uniquely yours.
- The purpose that energizes and sustains you.

You've begun to practise emotional mastery:

- Accurately naming what you feel.
- Regulating emotions so they serve you, rather than drive you.
- Owning the impact you have on people and culture.

You've committed to gathering feedback and used the Experiential Learning Cycle to improve your influence.

You've assessed your cultural alignment with your organization and have a plan to maintain or improve it.

You've learned how courage shows up in everyday leadership – how to embrace situations that make you uncomfortable or vulnerable when that's what's truly needed. You've recognized the environments and people that trigger fear, and you've begun to tame the inner voices that whisper inadequacy, letting fear inform rather than dictate your decisions.

You've seen how compassion – for yourself and for others – is essential for getting the best from everyone. You've practised listening deeply, demonstrating belief in people's potential and valuing their contribution to create an environment of flourishing.

Now you hold all the elements of Graceful Power, it's time to bring them together so they become your natural way of leading – in moments of challenge, in moments of opportunity and in the everyday interactions that quietly shape culture.

Modern leadership demands that we hold apparently opposing qualities at the same time: to be decisive yet open, confident yet humble, available yet boundaried. Leading with Graceful Power allows you to navigate these paradoxical expectations without exhausting yourself or diluting your impact. It gives you the steadiness to meet each situation with both strength and humanity.

The integrated mindset of graceful power

As you know, Graceful Power is not three separate skills; it's the weaving together of congruence, courage and compassion in real time.

- Congruence keeps you grounded in your values and aligned in your words and actions – even under pressure.
- Courage propels you into the conversations, decisions and actions that matter most, despite discomfort.
- Compassion ensures your leadership serves human needs as well as organizational goals.

When all three come together, you lead with authority that feels both strong and safe to others. Each quality acts as a counterbalance to the others, allowing you to stay centred in complexity, balancing opposing demands.

- Congruence anchors you when you must be both adaptable and principled.
- Courage enables you to take decisive action while staying open to new perspectives.
- Compassion lets you support people fully while also holding them accountable.

In combination, they turn tension into balance – and balance into forward momentum.

At the very beginning of this book, I shared how Allan Barton consciously evolved his leadership to bring more grace to his power. Denise Hatton's transformation travelled in the other direction. Her natural warmth, empathy and people-centred leadership were there from the start. But what changed everything was her ability to pair that deep care with structure, strength and strategic clarity – to bring power to her grace.

Case study: Denise Hatton – Bringing power to her grace

When I met Denise, she was entering her twelfth year as Chief Executive of YMCA England and Wales – the national body that serves, supports and represents the federation of independent YMCA member associations. She was justifiably proud of the impact the movement was having on young people's lives, and spoke with energy and care about the values that underpinned their work.

Recently, her team had revisited the YMCA's ethos statement, updating it to better reflect the lived culture of the organization. Alongside their existing value descriptors:

- We believe in the potential of all people.
- We go the extra mile.
- We do what we say and say what we do.

They added one more:

- We act with compassion and grace.

What pleased Denise most was that these new values weren't aspirational. They were simply giving language to something that already existed – something her team recognized and wanted to name. Behaviours like listening well, appreciating individuality and treating others with dignity were already part of the fabric. Naming them gave them more intention and allowed performance to be measured against them.

Denise is someone who leads with her heart. Purpose-driven and committed to helping young people thrive, her journey with the YMCA began when she took a weekend role supporting a housing project in central London. She knew within weeks she'd found her calling. Within months, she'd taken on a full-time position as a personal assistant to a regional leader. She rose through the organization, eventually becoming CEO of Dartford YMCA in 2003.

By the time she was appointed to lead YMCA England and Wales a decade later, the national body had experienced significant turbulence, with multiple chief executives across the previous ten years. Its culture was hierarchical, combative and driven by status and control. Though its role required transformation and deep change, many of the local leaders were reluctant to be led.

Denise was the only internal candidate to make the final shortlist – competing against a field of experienced, high-profile men from outside the movement. But the panel had the wisdom to recognize what the organization truly needed: not another forceful operator, but someone capable of rebuilding trust, strengthening the centre and modelling a different kind of leadership.

Still, Denise's leadership style – warm, collaborative and emotionally open – was at first misunderstood. To some, she looked soft. Others dismissed her as likeable but weak. A small group of influential, status-driven local leaders openly questioned whether she was tough enough for the role. Though buoyed by the confidence of her appointment, Denise found herself, 18 months in, facing serious self-doubt. The aggressive and personal criticism began to wear her down. She started to wonder: Did she have what it takes?

Instead of retreating or changing herself to fit the mould of her critics, Denise made a pivotal decision – she invested in coaching. Not to "fix" herself, but to understand herself more deeply and develop her leadership from the inside out. She wanted to lead with confidence – but on her own terms.

The coaching gave her the perspective, space and tools she needed to rebuild her confidence, refine her approach and reflect on the kind of team she needed around her. Rather than rushing to prove herself, she patiently assembled a senior leadership team that complemented her own strengths and aligned with the culture she was building. That team has remained with her – united around a shared vision of purpose, trust and human-centred leadership.

Together, they introduced strong structures and clear systems – creating the stability and transparency that allows the organization to remain adaptable, responsive and people-focused. This gave the space for care and compassion to flourish – not just as values, but as strategic assets.

Perhaps nowhere is this transformation more visible than in the YMCA's annual national conference. Once infamous for its adversarial atmosphere – so combative it was said there'd be "blood on the carpet" by the end of the day – the conference is now characterized by warmth, mutual respect and collaboration. National and local leaders engage, listen, challenge and support each other – united by a shared purpose and a renewed sense of trust.

What's most inspiring about Denise's story is not just the culture she helped create, but how she did it. She didn't silence her critics by becoming more like them. She chose, instead, to stay anchored in her values, to strengthen her leadership without hardening herself. She found a quiet conviction that allowed her to show up with presence and confidence – not in spite of her vulnerability, but because of it.

By deepening her self-awareness, facing discomfort with calm resolve and holding space for others with kindness and clarity, Denise brought power to her grace. In doing so, she created the conditions for others – her team, her peers and the young people her organization serves – to thrive.

Denise's story brings the qualities of Graceful Power into focus. Her journey to confident leadership saw her become even more fully herself. That's the essence of congruence – knowing who you are, what matters most and leading in a way that aligns with those values. Even when others questioned her, Denise remained anchored in her integrity, choosing not to mirror the combative behaviours around her, but instead to lead with clarity and consistency.

It also took courage – to face into criticism, to hold her nerve in the face of resistance and to take bold steps to reshape her leadership and the culture around her. Rather than shrinking under pressure, she sought support, deepened her self-awareness and made conscious, sometimes uncomfortable choices to lead in a way that felt right to her.

Throughout, compassion ran through everything she did. She built trust not through force but through care. She listened. She created the conditions for others to grow. Her leadership wasn't just about achieving results; it was about helping people – staff, peers and the young people they serve – to thrive.

Together, these three qualities didn't just transform Denise's leadership – they transformed the culture of an entire organization. Her story shows us what becomes possible when congruence, courage and compassion are actively practised.

You will have noticed that, like Denise, all the leaders in the case studies I've shared were not born with Graceful Power, nor did it come upon them by chance. The experience and wisdom gained across their career will have helped. But what made the real difference was their deliberate decision to improve their impact and expand their leadership by prioritizing the parts of their role that mattered the most.

A leadership discipline: Prioritizing what matters most

	Urgent	Not urgent
Important	I Tasks are both important and urgent	II Tasks are important, but not urgent (yet)
Unimportant	III Tasks are unimportant, but feel urgent	IV Tasks are neither important nor urgent

You may already know this time management tool, the Eisenhower Matrix, popularized by Stephen Covey in *The 7 Habits of Highly Effective People*.[1] It's a simple but powerful concept: all tasks fall into one of four quadrants, categorized by two measures – urgency and importance.

Covey's key insight is this: highly effective leaders spend most of their time in Quadrant II – the work that is important but not urgent. This is the work that builds opportunity, strengthens relationships and creates organizational resilience.

Quadrant II is also where Graceful Power thrives. It's the zone of thoughtful, intentional leadership – where reflection, forward planning, values-led decision-making and relationship-building take precedence over firefighting and constant reaction.

Making this shift isn't always easy. Transitioning more of your time and energy into Quadrant II means letting go of the short-term rewards: the satisfaction of "saving the day", the quick dopamine hit from clearing your inbox, the reassuring comfort of being the one with the answers. Many leaders have built their careers on being the most capable, the most responsive, the safe pair of hands. Stepping back from this can, at first, feel like stepping away from being valuable.

But as we've explored throughout this book, leading with Graceful Power isn't about doing more – it's about enabling others to do more by creating the conditions in which they can excel. The rewards are different here: slower to arrive, but far deeper and longer-lasting.

Only do what only you can do

Even within Quadrant II, not every important task needs you to do it. Here's a leadership mantra I share with all my clients: "Only do what only you can do."

Take a moment to let that settle in. Imagine confining yourself to the activities that *only you* can do – where uniquely your position, influence, experience or skill are required.

If a task can be done by someone else – even if you could do it faster or better – your role as a leader is to equip that person to succeed, not replace them. Every minute you spend on work that others could be doing is a minute you're neglecting the work that *only you can do.*

Exercise: Protecting time for what only you can do

Set aside 20–30 minutes in the next 24 hours to complete this exercise. The aim is to strengthen your time management boundaries – protecting and prioritizing the work that only you can do.

Step 1: Minimize distractions

Review your email, messaging and project management apps and their notifications.

- Identify what consistently pulls you away from focused, important work.

- Adjust your settings: silence non-essential notifications, unsubscribe from low-value emails, leave unnecessary groups.
- Automatically filter non-urgent correspondence for review daily or weekly and minimize the fragmentation of your attention.
- Harness technology to support your priorities, not sabotage them.

Step 2: Optimize how you spend your time

Review your calendar for the last 2–3 weeks.

- Which meetings or commitments truly needed your presence or direct contribution?
- Where did you add unique value – and where could things have progressed well enough without you?
- Notice patterns. Where are you pulled into work that isn't central to your mission and objectives?

Now look ahead:

- Which upcoming commitments can you delegate or decline immediately?
- What can you eliminate in the next few weeks and months with a little preparation?

Step 3: Protect your priorities

- Start with a blank week in your calendar – either digitally or on paper – and design the schedule you'd ideally work to going forward.
- First, identify the non-negotiable commitments, the timing of which are outside your control – for example, board meetings or cross-functional sessions.
- Then, schedule the activities that support your health and well-being – exercise, a lunch break, the time you stop being available for calls or meetings at the end of the day.

- Next, block time for the important, non-urgent work that only you can do: deep thinking, strategic planning, relationship-building, mentoring, opportunity creation – and your own development.
- Finally, release the remainder of your time for other routine meetings or impromptu conversations, safe in the knowledge that your most important work is already protected.

Where possible, align your schedule with your natural rhythms – using your peak energy hours for deep work and lower-energy periods for meetings or administrative tasks.

Let your colleagues know you're experimenting with how you manage your time, and invite their support and feedback. Be willing to make small adjustments for optimal impact, without eroding your boundaries.

When you focus your energy on what only you can do – and on what matters most – you lead not just with efficiency, but with intention, clarity and lasting impact. This is how leaders with Graceful Power create the space for others to shine while sustaining their own energy and influence.

Neglected leadership scenarios

In my experience, it's rarely the big, dramatic moments of leadership that define your influence. Far more often, it is how you handle the everyday interactions that are easy to postpone, avoid or overlook.

The following five common scenarios are frequently neglected, yet when you approach them with Graceful Power, they become opportunities to deepen trust, unlock potential and strengthen performance.

1. Designing and building effective relationships

Trust is the currency of influence. Without it, authority is fragile and short-lived. Yet many leaders dive straight into getting the work done and assume trust will grow automatically over time. They focus on tasks and delivery, rather than investing in understanding the people in front of them.

Graceful Power invites a different approach.

- Congruence means being authentic from the start – sharing who you are, what you value and what you stand for.
- Courage means setting clear expectations early and acknowledging that disagreements will happen, then designing together how you will handle them.
- Compassion means taking time to understand the other person's pressures and priorities, rather than seeing them only through the lens of what you need.

Start new relationships intentionally. Have a "working together" conversation – over coffee, on a walk or somewhere informal. Share your hopes for the relationship and invite them to share theirs. You will build trust more quickly and avoid many misunderstandings later.

2. *Having difficult conversations*

Unspoken issues rarely disappear; they usually grow. Addressing them early protects trust and strengthens performance, yet many leaders either avoid the conversation altogether or go in so bluntly that they overlook the impact of their words.

With Graceful Power, you bring clarity and care together.

- Congruence means being clear and specific about the intention and purpose of the conversation, rather than circling around the issue.
- Courage means describing the issue directly, without hiding behind vague language or excessive hedging.
- Compassion means making sure the person leaves with their dignity intact and a clear understanding of what needs to happen.

Begin with the end in mind. Before the conversation, ask yourself: "What do I want them to know, feel and do when we finish?" Let that guide your tone, your words and your energy.

3. *Career development discussions*

When people feel genuinely invested in, they become more engaged, loyal and ambitious. Yet development conversations are often treated as a formality, focused only on organizational needs or avoided altogether for fear of raising expectations you may not be able to meet.

Graceful Power helps you sit in this tension with honesty and care.

- Congruence means being open about both opportunities and constraints, rather than over-promising or shutting the conversation down.
- Courage means encouraging people to aim high, even if that may eventually take them beyond your team or even your organization.
- Compassion means listening deeply to understand their aspirations – not just in relation to their current role, but in the wider context of their life and career.

Offer curiosity before answers. Help them think aloud, reflect on what matters and explore possibilities. Where you can, make introductions or open doors that extend their network, knowledge and opportunities.

4. *Addressing underperformance*

Ignoring underperformance hurts both the individual and the team. Problems that stay unaddressed rarely improve; they tend to spread, negatively impact morale and erode trust. Yet many leaders hope an issue will resolve itself given time, or quietly compensate by doing the work themselves.

Graceful Power brings fairness, firmness and humanity together.

- Congruence means being even-handed and evidence-based, rather than relying on vague impressions or frustration.
- Courage means holding the person accountable for change, making it clear what needs to improve and by when.
- Compassion means separating the person from the performance – seeing their worth beyond the current problem and supporting them to succeed wherever possible.

Express belief in their potential at the same time as you hold them accountable. When people feel that your confidence in them is genuine, they are far more likely to commit to the effort required.

5. *Managing conflict with calm authority*

Left unmanaged, conflict drains energy and trust. Handled well, it can spark innovation, deeper understanding and real progress. Many leaders either avoid conflict, take sides too quickly or impose a neat solution without really listening.

Graceful Power calls you to a steadier, more skilful response.

- Congruence means staying anchored to shared goals and your own commitment to cultural values rather than being pulled into factions.
- Courage means facilitating the hard conversation, instead of sidestepping it or delegating it away.
- Compassion means hearing and acknowledging each perspective with care, even when emotions are running high.

Hold the belief that conflict carries value – that something important is trying to emerge. See the individuals as more than the disagreement and believe in their ability to find resolution with your support.

Exercise: From avoidance to action

Think of one leadership interaction you have been avoiding or neglecting. It might be a conversation, a relationship you have let drift, or a piece of feedback you have not yet given.

Ask yourself:

- Why does it matter?
- Which pitfalls are you trying to avoid – and what is the cost of continuing to delay?
- How can congruence, courage and compassion guide your approach in the situation?

Now make a specific plan: What exactly will you do and by when? Write it down. Then act.

Graceful Power is expressed less in grand gestures and more in what you choose to do with your time, attention and influence each day. When you protect time for the work that only you can do – and shift more of your energy into that important-but-not-yet-urgent Quadrant II space – you create the capacity to lead with greater intention. That space is what allows you to think ahead, build relationships and stay anchored in what matters most rather than being swept along by noise and urgency.

How you then use that space is what truly defines your leadership. The conversations you have (or avoid), the way you handle underperformance, the care you take with conflict, the interest you show in people's development – these "ordinary" interactions are where Graceful Power comes to life.

In the final chapter, we'll look outward – exploring the broader ripple effect of Graceful Power on your organization, your community and the world we share.

Chapter 14

The ripple effect

When you lead with Graceful Power, the benefits don't stop at your team's results or your organization's success. They ripple outward – shaping how people feel about themselves, how they work with others and even how they show up beyond the workplace.

A bigger vision

Imagine if more leaders led this way. Workplaces where everyone feels safe enough to speak up, confident enough to contribute their best and proud of what they're building together.

Organizations that measure success not just by financial results, but by how much they enable human flourishing.

Communities strengthened by leaders who bring clarity, courage and care to the decisions that affect them.

This isn't idealistic thinking – it's the natural outcome when congruence, courage and compassion become the standard for leadership. You've already seen it in microcosm: when you listen deeply, when you act with integrity under pressure, when you support someone's growth even when it's inconvenient – things change. Multiply that by hundreds, then thousands of leaders and the culture shifts.

Your reach is greater than you think

The influence of your leadership extends well beyond your job title. It shapes your relationships at home, in your community and in every group you touch. Each interaction is a chance to model a better way of leading – one that others can feel and want to follow.

People notice leaders who are both strong and kind. They notice the calm authority that doesn't need to shout, the openness that doesn't compromise standards, the confidence that doesn't demand the spotlight.

When they see it, it gives them permission to lead the same way.

An invitation

The work doesn't end here. In fact, this is just the beginning.

Graceful Power is a practice, not an end point. Some days it will come easily; other days it will feel like a stretch. Keep going. Each time you choose congruence over convenience, courage over avoidance, compassion over indifference, you strengthen not just your own leadership, but the environments you touch.

Share what you've learned. Mentor an emerging leader. Speak up in rooms where your voice can shape the tone. Build teams that don't just deliver results, but also restore people's faith in leadership.

The call to lead differently

The story of leadership is being rewritten. You have the chance to write your chapter – with grace and power.

Lead with conviction. Lead with care. Lead in a way that makes others want to do the same.

The ripple starts with you.

About the author

A world-class leadership coach with decades of experience, Sally Netherwood attracts leaders from around the globe: CEOs of major international organizations, radical entrepreneurs reinventing market sectors, influential activists advancing social justice and gender equality, celebrated creatives shaping culture and societal attitudes, non-profit leaders transforming the lives of disadvantaged communities along with policy-makers, pioneers and innovators.

Her mission is to demystify leadership development advice so modern leaders feel clearer, braver and more effective. A true catalyst for transformation, Sally draws on the insight gained from tens of thousands of leadership conversations to cut through the complex and often contradictory demands placed on leaders today. She reveals clear, tangible strategies, behaviours and actions that create immediate improvement in performance, workplace culture and daily working life.

Leaders who work with Sally are typically highly successful and privately aware that something more is possible. They come ready to be both challenged and supported, knowing that real growth demands courage, honesty and a willingness to change. This work is not for the faint-hearted, but for those who want to lead with greater influence, integrity and authority.

By discovering and embracing their Graceful Power, Sally's clients develop an inner strength and outward presence that enables them to achieve far more with significantly less personal cost.

Based in the UK, Sally works with organizations and individuals worldwide as a coach, consultant and speaker. **To find out more, visit www.sallynetherwood.com.**

Acknowledgements

Writing this book was only possible because of the many leaders who have trusted me with their triumphs and tribulations over the last 25 years. Without that trust, this book simply would not exist. Every client has a special place in my heart – I have learnt from you all and been inspired in countless ways. Thank you.

The writing itself did not come easily. My "process" involved more moaning, groaning and procrastinating than I care to admit. Reaching the finish line has everything to do with the encouragement and practical support of three people in particular: Sophie McKibbin, who spurred me on and never doubted I could do it; Alison Jones, my indefatigable publisher, who combined excellent advice with essential deadlines and Jenny Williams, who by committing to writing her own book *Brilliant Doubt* alongside me, became my writing companion – and someone to keep up with!

Many others gave their time, insight and encouragement as the idea of *Graceful Power* took shape. I'm especially grateful to Molly Aldridge, first champion of the Graceful Power concept; Anabel Hoult, who backed me so firmly I had no option but to follow through; Julia Ingall, who never stopped asking powerful questions and Carter Murray and Juliet Timms, the two most energizing cheerleaders.

My thanks also to Pam Burton and Ollie Thain for their thoughtful input on the original proposal and to my generous "beta readers" – Amy Brill, Hayley Gow, Jenny King, Mark Savage, Sonja Walde and Catherine Waton – who gave their time to read and provide valuable feedback on an early draft.

I am grateful for the expertise of the many people who contributed to the editing, design and production of this book: the teams at both Practical Inspiration Publishing and Newgen Publishing UK; development editor Ruth D'Rozario; copyeditor Rachel Cridland; project manager Kelly Winter; designer Ellen Walpole and illustrator Olimpio.

I am particularly indebted to the inspiring leaders who allowed me to pick their brains, some of whom appear as case studies in these pages: Kofi Amoo-Gottfried, Allan Barton, Simon Casson, Rebecca van Dyck, Denise Hatton, Clare Hornby, Bill Holroyd, Kathryn Morley and Helle Thorning-Schmidt.

Over the years I've been fortunate to collaborate with a number of outstanding leadership coaches, from whom I've learnt so much about myself and so become a better coach. With love and appreciation to Oona Collins, Joanna Kane, Pam MacIntyre, Julie Perrin, Sandra Richardson and Sandra Visser.

Beyond the writing desk, my thanks go to the Peregrine Rowing Club W3 squad of graceful and powerful women who keep me healthy and happy with their camaraderie on the Cam and all the friends who've picked me up and cheered me on as I wrote, especially Isobel, Debbie and Sally.

And finally, my family. Thank you to my parents, Tina and Peter, for never seeing a limit to my potential; to my mother-in-law, Shelagh, for her encouragement; to my sister Penny, a brilliant teammate through some difficult years; and to Antony, Noah and Wilkie – my absolute favourite people – for keeping me grounded, distracted and laughing.

Notes

The role of congruence in Graceful Power

[1] Gallup & Workhuman. *The human-centered workplace: Building organizational cultures that thrive.* Gallup (2024). Available from www.gallup.com/analytics/472658/workplace-recognition-research.aspx [accessed 18 August 2025].

[2] Elizabeth R. Brown, Curtis E. Phills, Joshua Kahn and Sadana Mukundan. *Feeling a sense of belonging is associated with more motivation within organizations that value diversity and equity.* Sci Rep 15, 23201 (2025). Available from www.nature.com/articles/s41598-025-04456-9 [accessed 13 November 2025].

Deepening self-awareness

[1] Michelle Obama. *Becoming.* (2018).

[2] James Sale. *Mapping motivation: Unlocking the key to employee energy and engagement.* (2015).

Developing authentic agility

[1] Lisa Feldman Barrett. *How emotions are made: The secret life of the brain.* (2017).

[2] Marc Brackett. *Permission to feel: Unlock the power of emotions to help yourself and your child thrive.* (2019).

[3] *How We Feel App*, developed by the How We Feel Project, a nonprofit started by Ben Silbermann and researchers including Marc Brackett.

[4] David A. Kolb. *Experiential learning: Experience as the source of learning and development.* (1984).

Understanding fear

[1] David Rock. *SCARF: A brain-based model for collaborating with and influencing others.* NeuroLeadership Journal, 1(1), 44–52 (2008). Available from https://schoolguide.casel.org/uploads/sites/2/2018/12/SCARF-NeuroleadershipArticle.pdf [accessed 14 June 2025].

[2] Alan Lew. *Be still and get going: A Jewish meditation practice for real life.* (2005).

[3] Marianne Williamson. *A return to love: Reflections on the principles of a course in miracles.* (1996).

The role of compassion in Graceful Power

[1] Stephen Trzeciak, Anthony Mazzarelli and Emma Seppälä. *Leading with compassion has research-backed benefits.* Harvard Business Review digital article. (2023).

[2] Jane E. Dutton, Kristina M. Workman and Ashley E. Hardin. *Compassion at work.* Annual Review of Organizational Psychology and Organizational Behavior, 1(1), 277–304 (2014).

[3] Zach Mercurio. *The power of mattering at work.* Harvard Business Review, 103(3), 100–109 (2025).

[4] Klodiana Lanaj, Remy E. Jennings, Susan J. Ashford and Satish Krishnan. *When leader self-care begets other care: Leader role self-compassion and helping at work.* Journal of Applied Psychology, 107(9), 1543–1560 (2022).

A mindset and a skillset

[1] Brené Brown. *Dare to lead: Brave work, tough conversations, whole hearts.* (2018).

Creating a climate of flourishing

[1] Amy Edmondson. *Psychological safety and learning behavior in work teams.* Administrative Science Quarterly, 44(2), 350–383 (1999).

[2] Charles Duhigg. *What Google learned from its quest to build the perfect team*. New York Times (2016). Available from www.nytimes.com/2016/02/28/magazine/what-google-learned-from-its-quest-to-build-the-perfect-team.html?smid=pl-share [accessed 16 June 2025].

Bringing it all together

[1] Stephen R. Covey. *The 7 habits of highly effective people: Powerful lessons in personal change*. (1989).

Appendix

My Code of Congruence

Values

I lead in alignment with my core values:

1.
2.
3.
4.
5.
6.
7.
8.
9.
10.
11.
12.

Future Self

A description of who I am becoming:

The guidance I received from my future self:

To accelerate my achievement of the qualities of my Future Self, I have committed to:

Letting go of these behaviours	Adopting these behaviours
1.	1.
2.	2.
3.	3.

My Leadership Signature

I am at my most inspiring and impactful
as a leader when I...

-
-
-
-
-
-
-
-

My Purpose Statement

Index

www.ingramcontent.com/pod-product-compliance
Lightning Source LLC
LaVergne TN
LVHW050955080826
845145LV00006B/1505

* 9 7 8 1 7 8 8 6 0 6 4 9 3 *